Writing up your research for a dissertation or thesis

The Quick Guide Series

By

Dan Remenyi & Frank Bannister

Academic Conferences and Publishing International Ltd
Reading
RG4 9AY
UK

info@academic-publishing.org

Disclaimer: While every effort has been made by the editor, authors and the publishers to ensure that all the material in this book is accurate and correct at the time of going to press, any error made by readers as a result of any of the material, formulae or other information in this book is the sole responsibility of the reader. Readers should be aware that the URLs quoted in the book may change or be damaged by malware between the time of publishing and accessing by readers.

This book mentions a number of commercial products, all of which are a trademark of their respective owners.

ISBN 978-1-908272-28-7

Available from: http://www.academic-publishing.org

Printed by Ridgeway Press

Contents

Preface

Producing a piece of academic research presents many challenges, two of which are acquiring the skill of academic writing and knowing what issues have to be addressed in each chapter of the finished dissertation or thesis.

Writing adequately for a research degree does not come naturally to most people. It is a learnt skill. It is difficult to acquire this skill and extensive practice is needed. It is therefore important that from the outset research degree candidates write about what they are doing and obtain advice from their supervisor/s at each stage of the research.

In addition, research degree candidates and their supervisors often have difficulty knowing when and where to stop the write-up of the research. There is a mystique about finishing doctoral dissertations and sometimes a researcher continues well after enough has been done to be comfortably awarded the degree. This can produce excessively long dissertations which then require reducing in size. Occasionally we have encountered two volume dissertations reaching nearly a thousand pages. You should not need so many pages to get a PhD in management or information systems.

Although this book is dense with regard to the information it contains, it has been designed to be read in four or five hours and it will give those who are preparing to finalise their research degree dissertation for submission a set of guidelines to follow.

The book can also serve those who may be interested in undertaking academic research and who do not know what the final output of their research will need to look like.

Readers of this book will realise that it is difficult enough to obtain a research degree when writing in one's own home language. Those whose first language is not English will find academic writing in this language all the more challenging. We have not specifically addressed issues related to the problems of writing in a second language.

Finally, we are aware that research degrees may be obtained by means other than a dissertation which is sometimes referred to as a monograph. One such approach is by published papers. This multiple paper and other approaches to writing up the research are not covered in this book.

Dan Remenyi

dan.remenyi@gmail.com

Acknowledgments

A book like this can only be written after many experiences with research degree candidates, with their supervision and their examination.

Many people have contributed to our learning over the past decade and we acknowledge our gratitude to all those we have worked with and learnt from. Learning by doing this is the only way of fully understanding what is required from research degree candidates.

Of course this learning continues and hopefully we can pass on some of the lessons we have learned to newcomers to academic research.

A key definition – the name of the book

There are two words which are sometimes used interchangeably to describe a document created to report the result of academic research presented for a degree. These are dissertation and thesis. Some universities prefer to make a distinction between these terms and when this is done the word dissertation is typically used to describe research at masters level. The word thesis is then reserved for the product of work conducted at doctoral level.

There is also the question of the different types of masters degree research. Traditionally, a masters degree was awarded for research which was neither as broad in scope nor as profound in depth as a doctorate. But it was clearly a research degree.

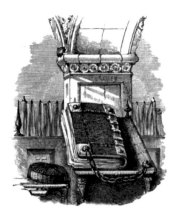

However, during the past two or three decades many if not most universities began offering masters degrees which were gained largely by course work and examination. Such degrees generally require only a modest amount of research work and the document written to report this research may be described as a minor dissertation, a research report, a project report or even a management challenge report.

If the term *thesis* is used, there is a different concern as the word thesis then refers both to the document or the book and to the contribution which the research has made to the body of knowledge.

Consequently, when the writer refers to 'this thesis', his or her meaning can be ambiguous.

Choosing words carefully is part of what is required from a skilled academic researcher. The best advice is to determine the conventional or required nomenclature in the academic institution to which the doctorate is to be submitted and to stick with that.

Besides the question of whether to use the word dissertation or thesis to describe the book which is to be submitted, there is the actual definition of the word dissertation (or thesis), something which is seldom addressed. A dissertation is a full and accurate account of the research which has been undertaken under supervision for the purpose of obtaining a research degree. A dissertation should specifically address the conceptualisation of the research question, the research processes and analysis, the findings, the conclusion and the application of the findings. It is expected that in the dissertation the researcher should demonstrate that he or she is aware of good practice related to academic research and that the work has complied with the research ethics protocol approved by the university.

Using this book to achieve your objectives

Remember that the purpose of the dissertation is to allow the researcher to show that he or she has added something of value to the body of theoretical knowledge. This means that the dissertation has to be written as an argument. The form of the argument is:-

- Demonstrate that there is a suitable problem or research question by reference to the literature and any other appropriate evidence;
- Choose a method of answering the research question;
- Implement the chosen approach to finding an answer;
- State what the results of the research are;

2

- Explain what the results mean to academics and to professionals;
- Indicate which aspects of the research you would do better if it were possible to repeat the work and make suggestions for future research.

This book has been written to assist researchers to achieve the above objective. It has not been written as a checklist or as a tool kit. Rather it treats this subject at a higher level, seeking to inform researchers of what is required to write up their dissertation by providing a better understanding of the objectives that they have to meet to be awarded a research degree. For this reason there are no charts in this book with boxes to tick.

Initially researchers may wish to read the book through from beginning to end and thereafter use it as a reference work for the different chapters in their dissertation.

Part 1 – Where to begin?

A research dissertation can be seen as having three major sections. These are the leading in pages (including the cover), the main body of the dissertation and the appendices.

This guide will address the main body of the dissertation first and then briefly discuss the leading pages and the appendices.

A research dissertation has a traditional layout which most research students follow. Few if any universities specify the presentation requirements for the dissertation, although most universities give research students specific instructions with regard to the cover of the dissertation and some of the leading pages.

Dissertations are traditionally presented in six chapters and these chapters are often named as follows:-

Chapter 1 – The Introduction

Chapter 2 – The Literature Review

Chapter 3 – Methodology

Chapter 4 – The Research

Chapter 5 – The Findings and Conclusions

Chapter 6 – Limitations and Future Research

The names of these chapters can and do vary. Sometimes, for example, the literature review chapter is called Theories, Concepts and Models – a name which some claim is a better description of the content of this chapter. The Methodology chapter may be named Research Design which some scholars argue is a more descriptive name for the material which needs to be addressed in this section.

The Findings and Conclusions chapter is sometimes presented as two separate sections and some dissertations will address the practical implications of the research in a separate chapter with a title such as Impact on Practice.

Examiners tend to like the six chapter model described above and if the researcher introduces more chapters then examiners may ask for the number of chapters to be reduced though this does not always happen.

There is no suggestion that the chapters listed above should be written in chapter number order. It is sometimes argued, for example, that Chapter 1, The Introduction, can only be written when the research has been completed because only then will the researcher fully understand what has been done in the research. Chapter 2, The Literature Review, requires updating throughout the research right up until the dissertation is about to be printed and submitted for examination.

There are also leading pages which appear before the body of the research and these are normally the:-

- Cover page;
- Abstract;
- Certificates of own work;
- Certificate of readiness to be included in the library;
- Certificate that the research has not been presented to another university;
- Acknowledgements;
- Dedication (if any);
- Other academic outputs;
- Table of contents;

- Tables of figures.

Some academics may, while under supervision, present their research at a conference or at a seminar or colloquium. If this has been done then a page named *Other Academic Outputs* may be included in the leading pages. In addition if the researcher has had a paper or papers published prior to submitting the dissertation it/they may be listed under this heading.

Universities have rules about which leading pages are required, the wording which should be used in them and what should appear on the cover of the dissertation. Research degree candidates should take care to follow all university guidelines of this nature as dissertations can be rejected by the postgraduate office (or the office of the director of research or whatever name the university uses) if the rules are not followed precisely.

There is usually a number of appendices after the final chapter. The List of References may be designated as an appendix although it is more typically separated and is effectively a section of the dissertation on its own.

Appendices may include among other things:-

- A glossary;
- Abbreviations and/or acronyms used;
- Questionnaire or interview schedule/s (if used);
- Data acquired in the form of either transcripts or numeric tables;
- The research protocol;
- Ethics protocol and correspondence thereto;
- Any other detailed explanatory evidence acquired during the research.

It is not appropriate to include in the appendices copies of papers presented at conferences or published in journals. A research degree candidate may bring such papers to the viva if he or she so wishes.

Unless there is a special reason for so doing, the appendices should not exceed 100 pages in length.

The number of pages which should be in the whole dissertation or thesis is difficult to prescribe. In most universities PhDs tend to have a permitted maximum of 80,000 words. This maximum can be, and is occasionally, exceeded. There is an informal consensus that 100,000 should be the upper limit. The number of pages this maximum constitutes is a function of the number of figures and tables in the work. However, 300 pages is a sound number at which to aim. After 400 pages concern will almost certainly be voiced that the work may be too long.

By the way, dissertations can sometimes be quite short. There are many stories about dissertations in mathematics being only a few pages long. Although this may well have happened from time to time, many of the stories told have an air of urban legend about them. In business and management studies a dissertation under 200 pages could be regarded by examiners as not constituting sufficient work for a doctoral degree.

Returning to the question of the maximum number of pages, examiners do not regard length (which requires the examiners to do more work, i.e. read more) as a contribution to excellence per se and thus examiners will not be encouraged to regard a piece of work as good simply because it is long. When a dissertation in excess of 80,000 words has been submitted, some universities will specifically ask examiners if they are prepared to accept such a long dissertation for examination and if the examiners refuse then the degree candidate will be asked to reduce the length of the work.

Before addressing the wide range of challenges involved in writing up research and preparing it for final submission, it is important to point out that this book is based on our experience across a number of universities and as such we have tried to make the advice as generic as possible. Every university has its own interpretation of the matters discussed in this book and as we have already mentioned (and will mention a number of times in what follows) the research degree candidate needs to find out the 'house rules' of his or her own university.

When to submit for examination

One of the great challenges which research degree candidates face is knowing when enough work has been done and when the dissertation is ready for submission to be examined. There is no easy way of determining when to submit. Regrettably there is no chequered flag. The submission decision is a question of academic judgement. However, there are some important guidelines which can help. To be awarded a doctorate the dissertation should provide a convincing argument that the research has resulted in something of value being added to the body of theoretical knowledge and this is referred to as the contribution of the research. The work should be presented in a scholarly way. It should be clear that the work is that of the research degree candidate. In business and management studies both a doctorate and a research masters degree should have some direct practical value for practitioners, which is sometimes referred to as management guidelines or implications for policy.

How does the research degree candidate convince himself or herself that this has been accomplished?

Firstly, although the supervisor or supervisors are not examiners in any formal sense they are de facto examiners. A dissertation should not be submitted without the backing of the supervisor. Secondly, the research degree candidate should have exposed his or her ideas to a number of different groups of people and obtained feedback. These groups may have been fellow doctoral candidates and other supervisors at colloquia or at seminars or workshops. The ideas may have been presented at a conference. The research degree candidate may have spoken to a professional or industry group about his or her research. He or she may have presented the findings of the research to a group of employees within one of the organisations which has been studied or who have shown interest in the research. If positive feedback has been obtained, then this is helpful in determining if the work is good enough to submit for examination.

In a similar way, some research degree candidates will have been able to have some of the ideas from their research published in a journal. A peer reviewed journal is ideal but for a research degree candidate to obtain feedback even a non-reviewed professional journal could be helpful.

Wittgenstein's (1969) remark:-

Knowledge is in the end based on acknowledgment

shows an insight as to how the academic research degree awarding process works. But there are problems with this approach, which involves what is generally referred to as academic judgement and is difficult to define. There is also the problem that there is little commonality as regards academic judgement which differs from person to person depending upon their background, their experiences and their culture. Even gender differences may creep in and affect academic judgement.

Part 2 – Writing the dissertation

Before discussing any of the questions concerning how to write academically, it should be noted that some individuals believe that they do not really know what they think about a subject until they write about it. This idea is similar to the expression normally attributed to E M Forster, "How do I know what I think until I see what I say?" The point is that expressing one's ideas with care causes one to focus attention on the subject in a more comprehensive way than engaging simply in quiet thought and this brings one's understanding to the fore. Articulating your ideas, whether verbally or in print, usually helps to crystallise your thinking.

In this book we are concerned with writing and academic writing does not come naturally to most people. It is different from report writing, brochure writing or letter writing. It is quite a different matter from writing a textbook or, for that matter, writing a novel. It requires a high degree of knowledge of the rules of academic writing and the ability to concentrate on both what is being written and how it is being written at the same time. This means that while the researcher is writing, he or she has to be simultaneously reflecting on how the material is being expressed. Not many people have a natural talent for this type of writing or can pick it up quickly. For most researchers this skill has to be mastered over a period of time. Traditionally research degree candidates have been told to develop the skills required to write academically by reading published papers in peer reviewed journals. Sometimes the dissertation of their supervisor is offered as an example. These can be helpful as reference documents, but they can also be confusing.

In a short insightful article Bertrand Russell points out that every individual has to develop his or her personal style of writing (www.gmarks.org/How_I_Write.html). Trying to imitate another person's style will simply not work. So don't try. This does not mean that lessons are not to be learned from reading works of successful authors, but imitation of style is not often helpful.

Obstacles to writing

There are several common obstacles that cause otherwise good and academically able researchers to struggle with their writing.

Probably the most common obstacle to producing a dissertation is a deep seated anxiety caused by the contemplation of the enormity of the task ahead. To those who have not written a dissertation already, the idea of an 80,000 word piece of work is daunting. A way of helping to ease this anxiety is to see the work as a series of distinct hurdles, each of which is relatively small, i.e. six manageable chapters instead of one large piece of work.

A second obstacle is motivation. Because of the perceived difficulty in writing the tome, some researchers postpone this task to the end of the research. This is a serious mistake. Leaving the writing to the end will mean that the demanding work of writing is unnecessarily concentrated and thus more painful. Not only that, but if a student has problems with academic writing, finding this out three quarters or four fifths of the way through the research could be disastrous. By writing sections of the dissertation as the research work is actually being done, the effort required at the end of the research becomes

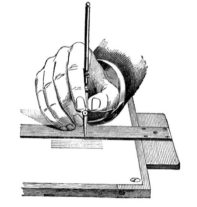

largely a compilation and editing exercise. So start writing your dissertation as soon as you can. If possible, from the first day you read a peer reviewed research paper, start making notes and save them on your computer together with the full reference to the paper or text book concerned. It is a good idea to put the references in the right format from the start (see notes on chapter 2 below). If you have found some words which you think will be useful to quote then remember to make a note of the page number.

Of course it is never entirely a question of compilation as there are important parts of the dissertation which can only be written at the end of the work. One of the ways of keeping the level of motivation up is to remind yourself continually of the value of the prize at the end. It is indeed considerable.

A third obstacle is the belief that long words combined in long sentences are important in academic writing. This is not the case, although it is correct to say that sentences can be too short and that you can end up producing something which is simplistic and that this is unacceptable. Furthermore, while short sentences are effective for getting across a message, they can make for an irritating prose style. Be aware that irritating an examiner is always a poor course of action! In general, you should write in language that is as clear and simple as is compatible with conveying the information or ideas that you wish to get across to the reader.

Another obstacle relates to the need for parsimony. One of the characteristics of acceptable academic writing is that it is parsimonious. Parsimony may be applied at a number of different levels and these include:-

- you should not repeat yourself unless such repetition serves a specific purpose (such as reminding the reader of a point that you made 50 or more pages back);

- you should get to the point quickly and not pad out an argument;
- long forms of a verb should not be used, for example - *he decided* should be used instead of *he made up his mind.*

Parsimony is best summarised as *Never say in a paragraph what can be said in a sentence.* It is not only a question of reducing long windedness; it also refers to not saying things which do not need to be said.

Being parsimonious does not mean expressing issues in the simplest possible way. Research degree candidates can sometimes write too simply. When this happens their work can appear to be 'dumbed down' and simplistic. A method for assessing if a piece of writing is written appropriately for academic presentation is the Gunning Fog Factor Readability Index http://gunning-fog-index.com/. Well written and easy to understand academic writing should not have an Index much above 20.

An integrated story

A dissertation has to tell an integrated story of why you are interested in doing the research; what other people have thought about your subject; how you thought about answering the research question; what actually happened; what it means; what its limitations are and what might be the next subject for you to research. Each of these topics is actually a story in its own right and needs to be told as such while retaining the overall plot of the complete dissertation.

Story telling is an art and it is difficult to provide guidance which is not considered trivial. John Steinbeck, who won the Nobel Prize for literature in 1962, famously said:-

"I have written a great many stories and I still don't know how to go about it except to write it and take my chances".
http://www.rjgeib.com/thoughts/steinbeck/steinbeck.html

From the earliest parts of our education we have been told that a story has to have a beginning, middle and end. Although this is true by definition, it is not always necessary that the beginning should be told before the middle and the middle before the end. The creativity of the author may allow these parts to be rearranged and some

great works start at the end of the story. Mary Shelley's masterpiece *Frankenstein*, where the story is told as a recollection of events, comes to mind as does Homer's *Odyssey* which begins in the middle of the story. In academic writing, on the other hand, the story needs to flow from beginning to end although a

brief summary is presented at the beginning in the form of the abstract.

Integrating the story of the research requires some planning of how it will be told. Many researchers produce a high level plan for the work which may be little more than a list of the chapters and the main issues which need to be addressed in each chapter. This list of chapters and notes may then be fleshed out and details supplied on a section by section basis. Some researchers find the use of diagrammatic representations such as brain maps or flow charts to be helpful. Others like to work in a less structured way and allow the story of the research to emerge as they write. The latter is probably only achievable, with few exceptions, by experienced academic writers.

Flow and continuity

An aspect of dissertation writing which many researchers find challenging is to create and maintain a flow of ideas and argument. Flow is similar to integration which has been discussed in the previous section but as well as implying a structured argument flow relates to the ease of reading and understanding. Ideas should be connected in a well expressed and easily accessible way so that a coherent argument emerges from the writing. This is a skill which has to be cultivated. The reader (and remember that this is the examiner) should never find him or herself having to ask a question such as: how did the researcher arrive at this point?

The use of the personal pronoun

Some researchers have difficulty in deciding when or whether to use personal pronouns in their writing. The first person plural, sometimes referred to as the royal 'we', should not be used in reporting academic research unless it is describing the actions or views of a number of people including the author and is thus the correct usage. In textbooks 'we' is often used in a way that is intended to include the reader (e.g. "we can thus see that..."). In a dissertation on the other hand, there is rarely any reason for using 'we'. The first person singular, i.e. 'I', is also best avoided, but may be used sparingly when any other construction is awkward. In general there is a clear preference in academic writing for the use of the passive and/or impersonal voice. For example, instead of writing "I used a positivist approach to the research" the same meaning may be communicated by the passive: "A positivist approach was used in the research" or active tense: "The approach used in this research is positivist".

One commonly encountered problem with the first person pronoun(s) is that it is increasingly argued that in qualitative research the researcher is required to state his or her personal position with regard to the research philosophy and that to do this it is necessary to use the first person singular. The use of the active voice here shows the researcher taking responsibility in a direct way. But here too, use of the first person singular is not necessary. Phrases like "The position taken..." or "The stance adopted..." can be used to convey the researcher's philosophical standpoint. Some researchers attempt to solve this problem by referring to themselves as "the researcher" or (worse) "the author". This tends to make the text sound stilted, as if the researcher were some abstract object out there. It should be avoided if possible and minimised if it cannot be eliminated. All of the above being said, there are no hard and fast rules provided the grammar and syntax are correct. The main consideration is that, whatever approach is used, the meaning is clear.

The tense of the verbs used - historical present

In English, when narrating past events, the present tense may be used. This form of writing is referred to as the historical present.

For example, in reporting research it is possible to write:-

When the manager arrived at the office he found that all the staff already knew that he had been fired.

or

When the manager arrives at the office he finds that all the staff already know that he is fired.

The historical present is used to create a more immediate and sometimes greater dramatic effect than a simple past tense.

However the historical present is not appropriate to describe the past in every instance. If a researcher is describing a fact about how the research was conducted such as: *All 20 questionnaires were sent to the XYZ organisation for distribution to their marketing staff*, this does not lend itself so well to the historical present transformation: *All 20 questionnaires are sent to the XYZ organisation for distribution to their marketing staff*.

The area of the dissertation where this question is probably most significant is the literature review. For example, one could write:

Smith (2003) argues that managers are slow to make decisions about this matter.

or

Smith (2003) argued that managers are slow to make decisions about this matter.

or

Smith (2003) argued that managers were slow to make decisions about this matter.

All three are acceptable though the third is potentially ambiguous as it implies that things might have changed since 2003. The important thing to note is that whichever style you choose, be consistent thereafter. A mix of past and present tenses can be jarring to read. Many researchers prefer the present tense, though this can sound odd when a reference is particularly old (e.g. "Newton (1687) writes that to every action there is an equal and opposite reaction."). Choose the style with which you are comfortable and stick with it.

Minimise the use of adjectives and adverbs

In daily speech communications there is a tendency to use (sometimes hyperbolic) adjectives and adverbs to describe individuals, processes or events. Often these are not necessary and they can lead to ambiguities. Words like *very, a lot of, superbly, genuinely* are examples. Such words should be eschewed in academic writing. It is a good idea to search for and remove superfluous adverbs and adjectives during the finalisation of the dissertation.

Acronyms/Abbreviations

Most dissertations will use some acronyms and it is important to define these before they are used. The correct approach is to supply the full version first followed by the acronym, for example, Grounded Theory Method (GTM).

Be careful of names and the use of conjunctions and prepositions as for example, the University of Reading uses the acronym of UoR.

Thereafter in referring to the matter for which the acronym has been stated only use the acronym.

The launch pad

Find an interesting starting point and compose an attention catching sentence with which to begin the writing. This is most important. You should be enthusiastic about your research and this enthusiasm needs to show in the way you write your dissertation.

Some researchers like to begin by sitting in front of their computer staring at a blank screen and then writing what comes into their heads. The story these researchers want to tell comes to mind as they write. This can work, though it is probably not the best approach for a newcomer to academic writing. It can though be useful for overcoming writer's block.

Another tactic is to develop a plan by taking a page for each chapter and listing the sections which will be addressed in that chapter. The subsections may then be listed within each section. This is called outlining and some teachers of writing skills refer to this as pre-writing preparation. Some researchers like to work in this way as they feel that they are creating a master plan for each chapter which helps prevent them from leaving anything out. Whether or not to use this technique is really a matter of personal style. Another line of attack that some writers find effective for a chapter is to write it out on a horizontal line with segments for each main part.

Diagrams, tables, figures and photographs

The terms diagram and figure are used interchangeably and the only concern here is consistency.

When used diagrams, tables, figures and photographs should be correctly numbered and referred to in the text of the dissertation by that number. It is useful to connect this number with the chapter number and thus the first diagram in chapter 3 will be Diagram 3.1.

A diagram may be of considerable value in affording an extra level of explanation to something that is being explained in text. However diagrams can become too complex and their explanatory power reduced or eliminated as a result. It is important to limit the amount of explanation delivered in one diagram. Sometimes where the matter is complex two diagrams may be necessary.

If appropriate a diagram may be presented in landscape form.

A diagram should be accompanied by text providing a proper explanation of the subject displayed and a diagram should not be positioned before the relevant text. Colour should be used with care as what appears attractive on a computer screen may not be so on paper. Some universities have internal rules about the use of colour.

The same sorts of rules apply to tables and figures. A table should not run over a page unless it is impossible to present the data otherwise. If it is essential, ensure that the headings are repeated on each page.

Photographs are normally allowed in dissertations, but they should be used sparingly and the reason for their use should be explained.

Where many diagrams, tables, figures and photographs are to be used then consider putting them in the appendix of the dissertation.

Some details of which to be careful

Pay special attention to definitions during the development of your arguments. Record what you consider to be suitable definitions from the literature. In compiling definitions do not use dictionaries or encyclopaedias unless all else fails. If you don't want to create your own definitions then find them in peer reviewed academic journals. Be careful what you assume about the knowledge of your readers, who are primarily examiners and likely to be reasonably erudite in the subject area of your research. For this reason do not define words which are in general use in your field.

It is virtually impossible to write any material amount of error-free text. All sorts of typographical errors creep in and although spelling and grammar checkers are quite good there are still many problems and errors which these tools will not catch. Punctuation problems, which can in extreme cases completely change the meaning of the text, can also occur. Therefore a dissertation should always be proofread. You should perform a first proofreading, but this needs to be followed by having another person read the work. Error blindness sets in when the author of a text reads it a number of times and thus a different set of eyes is always needed. Ensure this is the last task in the preparation of the dissertation and do not be tempted to add more text to the document after it has been proofread as this will introduce further errors that have not been checked.

References

Besides typographical errors there are often problems with the references which are notoriously difficult to present without error. These need to be checked as a separate exercise. Using automated tools such as *EndNote* will reduce this problem considerably, but can lead to other problems. There is always a trade-off when using automated tools such as reference and section numbering systems. These can simplify life considerably, but if they go wrong they can cause a major headache.

There is a number of different approaches to academic referencing. Among the most popular are:

- The Harvard Referencing System
- American Psychological Association (APA)
- Modern Language Association (MLA)
- Chicago Manual of Style

Except for the Harvard Referencing System these are described at http://owl.english.purdue.edu/owl/section/2/

These referencing systems are in general use and it is important that the research degree candidate knows the required system well and complies with it carefully.

There are also other systems such as the Oxford Standard for the Citation of Legal Authorities (OSCOLA). This is a specialised system for the legal fraternity.

There is a useful Harvard Referencing Tutorial at https://ilrb.cf.ac.uk/citingreferences/tutorial/index.html

Remember that examiners can be surprisingly picky and you do not want them to be able to criticise you for trivial typographical mistakes. Examiners sometimes say that if there are numerous trivial mistakes in the text then the degree candidate has not shown serious intent. Do not allow yourself to be put into this sort of situation and therefore remove all the typographical mistakes which will inevitably creep into your dissertation.

Be aware that one of the easiest places to make the typographical mistakes is in the reference list.

Copyrights and trademarks

One of the main reasons for paying meticulous attention to referencing is that the research degree candidate should not in any way infringe upon the copyright of another researcher or author. This is achieved by the recognition of the source of any ideas used or even alluded to in the dissertation.

Trademarks also need to be recognised and the symbol ™ after using the trademark is generally used to so do.

Scheduled writing

Some researchers find it useful to schedule a number of hours a week for writing parts of their dissertation from an early stage of the research. This can encourage a degree of discipline into the writing work and it keeps the matter of the writing in mind from an early stage.

Writer's block

All authors experience periods of greater and lesser productivity. Sometimes the productivity level is so low that it is better to stop writing. An acute form of this is writer's block. Writer's block can have a number of causes. One can be a problem with motivation. In this case focusing on the prize at the end of the work, as mentioned before, may help. Writer's block can also occur because the researcher is paralysed by not knowing how to start or how to approach what he or she wants to write. This is sometimes referred to as the 'deer in the headlights' problem. There are ways of dealing with this and good supervisors should be able to help the student with techniques and exercises to get around it. Many universities also have support services for academics and students with writing problems including writer's block. A third form of writer's block is where the researcher thinks that everything he or she writes simply is not good enough. A supervisor should be able to help with this problem. In an age of word processing and easy editing, this particular form of block is not hard to overcome. There is also a large number of websites offering advice on this subject.

Drafting and redrafting

The number of times a chapter of a dissertation requires re-drafting varies. It is unlikely that a dissertation, either in whole or in parts, i.e. chapters, will not have been re-drafted many times before it is submitted. It is not possible to attribute a value or number to the word *many* in this context. It is important to accept that you may well change your mind about how to express an idea, three, four or five times before eventually feeling comfortable that the idea has been expressed to your satisfaction. If you find yourself becoming despondent when redrafting your work yet again, just remind yourself that research degrees are challenging and that your achievement will be recognised and celebrated by many friends, family and colleagues. It **is** worth the effort.

Always keep copies of your earlier drafts. You never know when you might find it useful to reinsert that paragraph you deleted during the last revision. It is valuable to create and persevere with a rigorous version numbering and control system. Losing control of which is your most recent version can be troublesome.

Proofreading and editing

As a general rule no formal document should be submitted without proofreading and this applies to dissertation. Some authors are able to proofread their own work but this skill is relatively unusual. Most authors are too close to their work and when they try to proofread it they tend to read what they are thinking rather than what is on the paper or the computer screen. Because word processors have spelling checkers and grammar checkers many of the more obvious problems are today found by the computer but nonetheless many mistakes escape these devices.

Here is some advice which research degree candidates may find helpful:

Dissertations will generally need to be proofread a number of times and thus do not leave all the proofreading to the end. Proofreading should not be rushed and at the end of a research degree the candidates stress levels are often high and this make finding errors even more difficult.

Print out the text that is to be proofread. Reading from the screen tends to cause the mind to wander more than if it is being read on paper.

Remember you are looking for:

- Spelling mistakes;
- Typing errors including extra and missing spaces between words;
- Grammatical errors;
- Unnecessary repetition;
- Incomplete sentences;
- Punctuation problems;
- Diagrams, figures or tables which are not in the right place;
- Page number continuity;
- Undefined acronyms/abbreviations;
- Slang;
- Expletives;
- Errors in references.

Some tips to improve the finding of errors:

- Read the text slowly;
- Re-read each line before moving on to the next one;
- Point with you figure to each word as you read it;
- Read the text out loud;
- Use a ruler or a blank page to cover up the oncoming text;
- Proofread for different type of mistakes which occur regularly;
- Do not allow yourself to become too tired as this will cause you to miss mistakes;
- Ask a friend or colleague to proofread the document with you – each of you reading alternative pages perhaps.

The errors found during the proofreading have to be corrected with care as corrections may cause additional errors. Use track changes so that you can review the changes.

Do not underestimate the time it will take to perform a competent proof reading exercise.

Proofreading is not the same as editing. Proofreading only involves pointing out where errors are. Proofreading may suggest some minor improvements to the writing, but it does not involve any redrafting. Editing, on the other hand points out errors, but in addition an editor will change the text in order to clarify the meaning.

Some universities do not allow a researcher to have his or her work edited except under exceptional circumstances The following extract from the Rules of Trinity College Dublin is informative.

> *"The use of paid professional copy editing services for the preparation of a Masters or doctoral thesis is **not permitted** [the bold and large type face is from the College document] and will be considered a breach of the examination regulations. In certain exceptional cases, students registered with the College disability service may, following consultation with the Dean, be permitted to avail of paid professional copy editing services."*

Learning to write academically

It is important to realise that competent academic writing cannot be learnt from a book or in a lecture. Academic writing is one of those skills which can only be learnt by working alongside an accomplished practitioner. It has to be learnt slowly with many trial and error attempts over a considerable period of time.

An ideal way to develop this skill is to find an experienced academic who will allow you to write with him or her, for example on a paper for submission to a journal. As this may be difficult to achieve, the next best strategy for learning is to have your supervisor evaluate written material regularly. As noted above, this is particularly important in the early stages as failure to get the writing style right from the start can mean unnecessary re-writing and editing later on.

You can also obtain more feedback by entering into a reciprocity arrangement with other researchers so that you read each other's work and offer each other suggestions.

Another important learning technique is to pay attention to the style and not just the content of the literature you are reading (see Chapter 2). Good journals have strict rules about the quality of the written English that they publish and there is nothing wrong in learning by imitation when it comes to writing style (provided you do not plagiarise the content, of course).

Start working towards improving your writing as soon as you can as it will take time. When you are recognised as writing well you will certainly obtain a high degree of satisfaction from this achievement and so you should.

University rules for producing the written document

Universities have specific rules about how the document should be produced and these rules can address the font or typefaces which may be used and the font sizes which are considered appropriate. The colour of the print is often specified as black. Some universities regulate the colour which may be used in diagrams. It is usually the case that only one side of the paper may be used. In a recent examination a degree candidate used the back of the preceding page for a diagram and one of the examiners objected to this. In this case it transpired that the degree candidate had consulted the post graduate examination office and that it was permissible at that university to print diagrams on the back of the preceding page.

The rules may also include margins, number systems, styles of heading, justification and use of foot- or endnotes. The following is an extract of the Thesis Submission Guidelines for Students for Trinity College Dublin, August 2011:-

The thesis must be printed on good quality, A4 (297 x 210mm) white paper. The type must be fully formed as in the output of a laser or ink jet printer. The output of dot matrix printers is not acceptable. The type must be black and not less than 10 point. Line-spacing must be at one and a half or double spacing between lines. The gutter margin of both text and diagrams must not be less than 35 mm and that on the other three sides not less than 20 mm. The two copies of the thesis for examination should be soft-bound and printed on one side of the page only. It is required that the hard-bound copy of a thesis will be printed on both sides of the page on paper of a weight of at least 90 gsm (exceptions are at the discretion of the Dean of Graduate Studies). A copy of the hard-bound thesis will be lodged in the Library following approval by Council. Colour photocopies and scanned images may be used in the copy of the thesis deposited in the Library.

Some universities/faculties/schools allow footnotes to be used while others do not. Notes at the end of a chapter are sometimes allowed (these are referred to as endnotes and need to be distinguished from the software product of that name). Researchers are advised to determine the rules of their institution. However in general footnotes and endnotes should be minimised as some examiners do not feel that they are helpful.

Some examiners have complained when there has been extensive use of foreign expressions, for example, Latin phrases such as *ab initio, ipso facto, a concrario* and *pari passu*. Expressions such as these should be used with caution.

American words and expressions are creeping into the English language, as they have done for hundreds of years. Recently the following was found, 'He was called away to an urgency!' and 'He was credentialed by the Professional Institute'. The word 'alphabetize' is used in place of sorted alphabetically. Expressions like these need to be avoided.

American spelling is also a problem. In general American spelling is unacceptable in English academic work. So, ensure that the English version of the software is in use and the spellchecker software should be inspected and set accordingly.

It is the research degree candidate's responsibility to establish what these rules are for his or her own university and comply with them exactly. Examination offices have been known to reject dissertations for the smallest infringement of these rules. There is also the question that an external examiner may not know the rules and, as in the case above, be incorrectly critical of the student.

The result of the dissertation

Many universities simply record as the final result of the doctoral (or masters examination) that a dissertation has been accepted and that the degree is awarded with no grade attached to the work, i.e. no comment is made with regard to a First or other level of pass. But some universities do award distinctions or use more interesting terms such as cum laude, summa cum laude or magna cum laude. There are also other ways in which an extremely good piece of work can be recognised such as dissertation competitions. The Chartered Institute for Information Technology has an annual award, as do the American Academy of Advertising and The Association of Operations Management, to mention only three of many such competitions.

Learning sources for academic writing

There is a number of resources available on the web to assist learners acquire the skill of academic writing. These range from full courses to a range of grammar checkers to spellcheckers to dictionaries and thesauruses.

Pearson has a new product to be launched in 2012 called MyWritin-gLab Global which is a full course in English writing with various testing facilities included. Individual students may enrol directly with this website.

Getting to the end

By the time most research degree candidates hand in their disserta-tion they are glad indeed that they have reached the end of this educational journey. The work is not only challenging, but it is quite hard to sustain the enthusiasm for the project which may have taken three or six years or even longer. So don't feel that you are different if you are delighted to have finished and handed it in. Just remember that the examiners may require some more work from you. However, if you have been diligent and your supervisor has been attentive then the additional work should not be too substan-tial.

Part 3 – The main body of the dissertation or thesis

The first chapter - introducing the research

Chapter 1 sets the tone for the whole work and as such it is of critical importance that it is well crafted to demonstrate the scholarly skill of the researcher. The opening paragraph needs to catch the attention of the reader and the subsequent paragraphs need to be able to retain it. This chapter is usually called The Introduction, but other titles are possible such as The Starting Point. Some academics suggest that Chapter 1 should be written when all the other chapters are finished. Others suggest that writing a full draft of this chapter helps you settle in and get the writing process started. Whichever approach you adopt, Chapter 1 will either need writing or updating when the rest of the dissertation is finished. It can also happen that the nature of the research question changes subtly (or sometimes not so subtly) during the literature review. For example, a researcher may find that the question has already been answered or that there is a more interesting question to investigate. Should this happen, anything already written in Chapter 1 would need to be updated in the light of this. In some universities a change in the research question is treated as a minor matter which may be dealt with by the research degree candidate and the supervisor without any other formalities. At other universities a change in the research question requires a resubmission of the research proposal as well as a new ethics protocol.

Chapter 1 has four important functions and these are to explain to the reader:-

- the nature of the questions which are going to be researched. In so doing it should address some of the background to the field of study. This might include a description of the industry in which the research will take place or other dimensions of the context of the study;
- why answering the research question(s) is important and to whom it is important. This is sometimes expressed as demonstrating the relevance of the research;
- in general terms, what the approach to the research will be;
- what the results of the research deliver.

It is important that the researcher shows that he or she is aware of the requirement for an ethics protocol and what needs to be done about obtaining approval from the university ethics committee.

It has become customary for chapter 1 to end with a list of the other chapters which will be addressed in the dissertation.

It is important not to exceed 12 pages in achieving the above. Parsimony is important in all academic writing and this chapter is a good place to start developing the habit of writing parsimoniously.

In chapter 1 it is appropriate to make reference to a small number of important or seminal published works, but it is really quite important that the author does not allow this chapter to become part of the literature review. A similar point can be made concerning the general terms in which the research approach is discussed.

Some universities like to see a section in Chapter 1 called delimitations. This is not the same as limitations. The word delimitations refers to the scope of the research. There are pros and cons as to the benefit of such a section, but it is not essential.

In general nothing should be said in the dissertation which is not relevant to developing the argument that your research contributes something of value to the body of theoretical knowledge. It is especially important not to make statements which are repetitions of well known and agreed opinions (often referred to as motherhoods).

This chapter should be summarised with a strong statement of the relevance of the research. However, it is important that the research degree candidate does not oversell the importance of the research finding(s).

Unlike what sometimes happens with undergraduate essay assessment, every word in your dissertation will be read by your examiners who will definitely ask, "Are these words the most appropriate way of saying this?" and "Are these words necessary?" So you really need to be critical of your own writing and make sure that everything you write is there for a reason and that it lends weight to the argument that you are developing.

The second chapter - what is known about your topic

Chapter 2 builds on the material to which the reader has been introduced in Chapter 1 and it explores it in considerable depth. The depth required is such that this chapter should make it clear that the researcher has a comprehensive understanding of all the scholarly work already published in his or her chosen field of study.

Academic research is based on the principle of scholarship. Scholarship has a number of dimensions, one of which is that the scholar needs to be fully familiar with the academically published material in the field of study as well as relevant material from the world of practice (if any). The scholar needs to be able to use this knowledge to explore an important question and craft a convincing argument relating to that question. One of the hallmarks of a convincing argument is that it has been developed as a result of a critical review of the literature.

There are three major dimensions to a literature review for an academic research degree:-

- The review needs to be comprehensive which means that all the important papers in the field of study need to have been read and commented on.
- The literature reviewed should mostly have been published in peer reviewed academic journals and these should be journals which are highly regarded by academics in the field of study. Open access journals are increasingly acceptable, although the number of these used needs to be monitored. A small number of references can be made to non-peered reviewed sources and practitioner or other sources, but these need to be minimised and their relevance justified with care.
- The literature reviewed must encompass the contemporary literature. The definition of contemporary will vary from one field of study to another and there will be a degree of variation from one scholar to another. In general, contemporary is understood to mean published within the last five years. Note, however, that not all important papers will be contemporary in this sense. Older seminal papers should be referenced, but such earlier papers should be chosen for

their continuing relevance or for the need to have a foundation point from which to start understanding the topic.

An important question is where the literature review should begin. In some fields of study there may be one or a small number of seminal papers which can constitute an interesting and useful starting point. Alternatively, there may be a recently published paper which attempts to overthrow or challenge traditional thinking in the field. Wherever Chapter 2 begins, it is important that it addresses both seminal papers and right up to the minute current thinking. It is necessary to say that even after this chapter has been written and submitted for examination, the researcher is expected to keep up to date with what is being currently published until the awarding of the degree has been signed off by the examiners.

In order to produce an appropriate literature review at research masters or doctoral level it is necessary to understand the different levels of thinking which need to be brought to this task. A literature review can be done at four levels of sophistication. For a PhD the researcher needs to have incorporated all four levels. These levels are:

- Reportage - this is when the content of each paper is reported or précised. This can be useful to get a grip on the literature and many students will summarise papers in order to understand them (and to be able to recall them later).

- Critique - this involves assessing the strengths and weaknesses of the ideas in the paper, for example pointing out gaps or inadequacies in an argument. This is your own judgement on what you are reading. Researchers are required to demonstrate their skills at critique which needs to be made clear from the manner in which the literature is reviewed.
- Consolidation - at this stage you bring together what you have read, explore where there is agreement or disagreement, compare and contrast different theories or conceptions, examine contradictions in argument or evidence. You may classify the literature into appropriate groupings.
- Synthesis - this is the most challenging step as it involves reflection and judgement. Here the researcher draws from the full body of existing scholarship. This normally leads to, or back to, the research question.

Chapter 2 does not consist of a simple historical account of papers published on the topic and if you present it this way, the examiners are likely to send it straight back to you. It should categorise papers by schools of thought and show how thinking has developed over the years. There may have been disputes and arguments among researchers and if so, this should be highlighted. Where the topic is interdisciplinary in nature, a literature review from both disciplines will need to be undertaken and the researcher needs to be careful about how the connection between the two fields of study is shown.

Chapter 2 has seven important functions. These are to explain to the reader:-

- the depth and breadth of knowledge in the field of study of the researcher;

- the prior research which has had most impact on the researcher's thinking;
- the critical ability of the researcher;
- the researcher's ability to craft an argument;
- the location of the research question within the context of the literature and existing scholarship;
- the articulation of the research question;
- what previous attempts (if any) have been made to answer the research question.

The size of the body of literature which needs to be addressed is a function of how much interest the research area has attracted over the years. At masters level a research degree candidate would be expected to have consulted 50 to 100 references while at doctoral level the number is probably in excess of 200 or 250. Where the research is at the intersection of two large fields, the number of references may top 300 or even 350. The majority of these, say 75%, should be contemporary and a similar number should be from well regarded peer reviewed journals. The website for the Association of Business Schools keeps a list of journals which are ranked on a four star (best) to one star basis. Peer reviewed books and conference papers are also important. Non peer reviewed books can be important too, especially if they are widely cited. As well as academic sources, a literature review may also encompass documents produced by institutions such as the OECD or the World Bank.

Do not rely too heavily on verbatim quotations from others. A small number of these may be useful, but it is necessary to limit them. Lengthy quotations (more than a few lines) should be avoided unless they really are important to your argument or illustrate a critical point.

Sometimes flow charts or Venn diagrams are useful in this chapter – especially if it is long (more than 50 pages).

Where a new field of study is being explored the approach described above will need to be modified. A new field of study will not have as great a breadth or depth of peer reviewed literature on which to draw as a well established topic. When this occurs it will not be possible to find the same quality and quantity of established thought on which to develop new academic research and as a result the researcher may have to rely on less academic material such as non-peer reviewed publications. In business and management studies this would mean that newspapers such as The Economist, The Financial Times or The Wall Street Journal could be used as references. In fast moving fields such as ICT or IS, it may also be necessary to include references from the Web, but these should be used with great care.

It is important that the researcher uses this chapter to reinforce the argument that the research is relevant to current academic and practitioner needs.

Chapter 2 may be summarised by the researcher indicating which of the authors referred to in the literature review have had most influence on his or her thinking. Put colloquially, on whose shoulders does the researcher see him or herself standing?

Finally, it is essential that the researcher is aware of the referencing style used by the faculty or school and this needs to be rigorously applied throughout the work.

This chapter is normally between 40 and 60 pages in length.

As implied above, this chapter cannot be fully finalised until the end of the research so the researcher will probably go through numerous versions of it before the degree is awarded.

Where there is an interdisciplinary/ multidisciplinary / trans-disciplinary /cross-disciplinary dimension to the research question it will be necessary to incorporate more than one body of published papers into the literature review. Some researchers choose to separate these different bodies of knowledge and present the literature in two or maybe even more separate chapters. Many (though not all) examiners do not approve of this as they argue that there is one major research question and this should be seen in the light of one argument arising out of an integrated or synthesised view of the literature. However, it can be a challenge to bring together a synthesised view from more than one body of published knowledge and dividing the literature into multiple chapters is one way of avoiding this problem.

The third chapter - how the research will be done?

Chapter 3 opens with the re-statement of the research question. Research questions are normally expressed at a high level and to be tractable, the question usually has to be reduced to a number of sub-questions.

This chapter provides the researcher with an opportunity to demonstrate his or her depth of knowledge of research philosophy and how that knowledge impacts on the choice of research design. A discussion of the philosophical justification for the choices made is useful. Those who are studying for a PhD will relate to the importance of some philosophical knowledge (as the word 'philosophy' is in the name of the degree they are seeking), but even those who are working towards a professional doctorate such as a Doctor of

Business Administration (DBA) are required to show a modicum of philosophical knowledge. Notwithstanding this, it needs to be remembered that it is a doctorate in business and management studies which is being sought and not a doctorate in the subject of philosophy. Too much philosophy will detract from the value of the dissertation.

The following are some of the philosophical questions which the researcher needs to consider:-

- Am I taking a realist or a social constructivist point of view?
- Is the research to be based on a theorist or an empiricist approach?
- Will positivistic or interpretivist methods of evidence collection, or a mixture of both, be used?

and

- To what extent does the researcher consider himself or herself a pragmatist?

If you are taking one of the less common philosophical or ideological stances, such as a critical theory approach, this will need to be explained and defended. Do not engage lightly with unusual approaches, particularly with a critical theory approach as it has detractors who are strongly sceptical about it and you may find yourself having to defend your position against robust attack in the viva.

Some researchers feel that once they have heard a new word and obtained a rudimentary understanding of its meaning it may be used in the dissertation. This is not so.

It is important if the researcher uses any of the terms described above that he or she is fully conversant with its meaning. If a viva or a defence is involved then the researcher needs to be able to answer a question such as: *"What are the principal approaches to interpretivist research and what are their strengths and weaknesses?"*

The mainstream of business and management research follows a realist perspective. Traditionally, research in this field was largely positivist and empiricist. Although the term pragmatist was not extensively employed, the fact that business and management researchers were concerned with delivering something of value to both academics and practitioners effectively meant that there has always been strong undertones of pragmatism in academic business research. Pragmatism is now experiencing a revival and is being more clearly articulated as a distinct research philosophy, although there are still academics who have difficulty with this philosophical approach.

Although much is made of the differences between quantitative and qualitative research, and individuals who support quantitative or qualitative approaches often engage in what can become acrimonious debate, virtually all academic research projects in the social sciences require both quantitative and qualitative data. A simple example of this is that even when a questionnaire is to be used to acquire the data, the form and the content of the questionnaire can only be finalised after some qualitative discussion in terms of the data requirements and how they will fit into the process of answering the research question. Furthermore, when the analysis of the data obtained from the questionnaire is complete, the process of understanding and interpreting the findings is essentially a form of qualitative research. Thus in a sense it may be said that there is an element of mixed methods in all academic research.

As mentioned before, once the research question and its subquestions have been finalised, the data which will be required to answer the research questions will normally be obvious. When this is known then the method of data acquisition and the techniques required to analyse it should become clear. This process is shown in Figure 1.

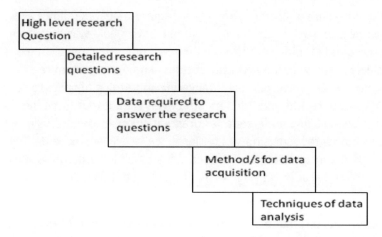

Figure 1: The steps from high level research question to data analysis

The logical chain from high level research to data analysis is an important one both from a philosophical point of view and from a practical viewpoint. The connection between these steps can become disjointed and this can lead to serious errors creeping into the research process. Note that there may be several possible methods of data collection and data analysis.

There is an important distinction to be made with regard to how quantitative data, as opposed to qualitative data, is collected. Quantitative data could be financial statistics published in a set of annual accounts or share prices quoted on the stock exchange. Quantitative data could be the throughput of particular types of machines or it could be the number of items rejected by quality control each hour or it could be the rate of pay of various individuals. Also qualitative data may be collected using a questionnaire. Where a questionnaire has been used, Likert Scales are often employed and if this is the case then the researcher will have to carefully explain and justify the method which will be used to analyse data of this kind.

In this last case quantitative data will be collected using a previously validated measuring instrument such as a questionnaire which will have been pre-tested and field-tested. The questionnaires are completed by informants and then collected. The data is then managed by the researcher before the analysis begins. In this case the research process is continuous as shown in Figure 2. An important point here is that the detailed questions cannot be changed after the questionnaire has been published or circulated.

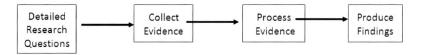

Figure 2: The processes of quantitative academic research

When using qualitative data such as interviews the researcher is involved in a learning experience in which he or she can improve their data collection technique as well as add new detailed questions or omit a not so useful question from the interview schedule, if necessary, at any time. This opportunity which is inherent in qualitative research is shown in the feedback loop in Figure 3. In certain circumstances, it may even be possible to re-interview earlier informants in the light of subsequent evidence. One research approach, the Delphi method, explicitly uses this process of revisiting earlier informants in the light of findings from the earlier rounds of interviews or questionnaires.

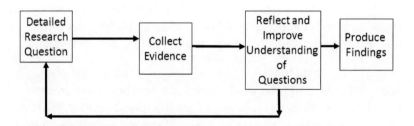

Figure 3: The processes of qualitative academic research

Having settled the research question/s, this leads to being able to establish the data required to be able to answer the question/s.

It is often the case that the research question can be answered from different perspectives and this may mean that different types of data will be required. It is important to state which perspectives the researcher is addressing and why these perspectives were chosen. This may lead to a discussion whether the research approach should be considered as mixed methods. This discussion should also clarify whether the research will be conducted deductively or inductively.

Identifying the data required will lead to a position from which it is reasonably clear what type of analysis would be appropriate. For academic research the researcher will need to specify how the data will be collected and managed. Then it is necessary to discuss how the chosen analytical techniques will be applied and what their results will mean.

Where data is to be collected using a sample (as opposed to, say, interviewing everybody in an organisation), the population, sampling frame and method of selecting the sample need to be worked out. Some people occasionally refuse to be interviewed; a particular (and common) problem with questionnaires is low response rates. The researcher will need clear strategies to handle these matters and to be able to demonstrate that he or she has followed good practice. Problems relating to potential biases and what the researcher intends to do about these also need to be addressed. An account of how triangulation could help with overcoming these difficulties is commonly provided.

If interviews are used, then the researcher needs to discuss access to individuals, snowballing (if used) and field note taking. Snowballing is quite a common practice in interview based research. It is important to be able to demonstrate that this does not result in a significant degree of bias. The number of interviews undertaken has to be justified and this needs to be done by reference to data saturation.

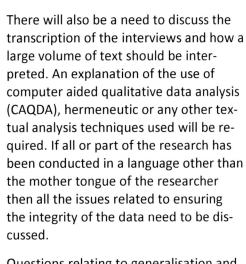

REACHING
AFTER
KNOWLEDGE

There will also be a need to discuss the transcription of the interviews and how a large volume of text should be interpreted. An explanation of the use of computer aided qualitative data analysis (CAQDA), hermeneutic or any other textual analysis techniques used will be required. If all or part of the research has been conducted in a language other than the mother tongue of the researcher then all the issues related to ensuring the integrity of the data need to be discussed.

Questions relating to generalisation and replication and validity, or their qualitative research equivalents such as creditability, transferability, dependability, confirmability or authenticity should be discussed.

This chapter requires the researcher to

justify the methods that will be used. It is also necessary for the researcher to show evidence of knowledge of the other methods which could have been used and why the chosen one was superior to, or at least as good as, any of the others. In some cases the best method may simply not be practical and if this is the case, why this is so needs to be explained clearly.

The importance of this chapter is that it provides the justification for the researcher's claim that he or she has made a contribution to the body of theoretical knowledge. Do note however that this claim will be discussed in full in the following chapters.

Although not strictly an ethics consideration itself, the ethics protocol can directly influence some of the method choices and thus this needs to be addressed here.

Towards the end of this chapter, hypotheses, propositions or conjectures would be stated if some sort of theory testing was to be performed. If theory discovery was the focus of the research then the details of a grounded theory method (GTM) or other appropriate approach would need to be provided.

In addition to a discussion of positivism/interpretivism/critical research and quantitative/qualitative research, something that is occasionally found in Chapter 3, as a sort of hygiene factor, is an overview and/or brief review of *all* of the common business research techniques (at least as far as data acquisition is concerned). As noted above, it is essential to discuss any reasonably plausible approaches to the research which have not been used. It is not necessary to discuss methods which are not relevant or clearly impractical. However, as a PhD candidate you will still be expected to know something about these other methods and, even if they are not discussed in your dissertation, they may come up in a viva or defence. The following is a list of methodologies and research techniques with which every doctoral student in business and management should be at least broadly familiar:

- Surveys/questionnaires;
- Experiments;
- Focus groups;
- Interviews;
- Grounded theory method;
- Action research;
- Ethnography;
- Participant observation;
- Delphi Method;
- Historiography;
- Document/archive research.

You are not expected to be familiar with every arcane method or research tool in the repertoire, but knowledge of the list above is strongly recommended.

If you claim that your research employs mixed methods then it is necessary for you to provide a justification for this approach both on a philosophical and an operational level. Although this is not difficult neither is it trivial and a sound argument needs to be crafted for this course of action.

The summary of this chapter should include a strong statement demonstrating that the researcher knows the importance of research rigour and has attended to all the concerns which make the research rigorous.

This chapter is normally between 30 and 50 pages in length.

Although true to some extent of every chapter in a doctoral dissertation, Chapter 3 in particular has the dual purpose of ensuring that the researcher explains his or her understanding of the philosophy/methodology to the examiner as well as sorting out these ideas for himself or herself.

Chapter 3 is usually called Research Methodology or Research Design.

The fourth chapter - an account of the research- what was actually done?

Chapter 4 is an account of what was actually done during the research and what results were obtained. Therefore this chapter will largely follow the proposed course of action which was laid out in Chapter 3. Of course the execution of the research may differ at times from the proposed research design described in Chapter 3 and where this has happened it should be directly addressed and the reasons for the variations discussed.

As a high level general statement it is possible to say that if quantitative research was undertaken then the main framework of the research process will probably be deductive whereas if qualitative research is used then the main framework will probably be inductive. There are  exceptions to this which will be discussed later.

The structure of this chapter will depend on two factors. First it will reflect whether the primary aim of the research is to develop a new theory (or extend an existing theory) or whether it is to test an existing theory. Secondly it will depend on whether the approach is quantitative, qualitative or a mixture of both. In the latter case it will need to reflect how these two approaches were combined (e.g. what is the balance between them and in which order were they undertaken). For quantitative researchers, if a bespoke questionnaire was used, then the researcher should provide an account of how the questionnaire was developed using focus groups, interviews and pre- and field-testing as well as some initial data analysis. These activities would then constitute the researcher's claim that the questionnaire was a validated measuring instrument.

If a previously developed questionnaire is used, then the source of the questionnaire needs to be stated and its selection justified. A previously validated research instrument will reduce the amount of work to be done, but it is important to remember that in doctoral research you have to add something new. Merely re-cycling an unmodified existing questionnaire is unlikely to be enough.

Where the questionnaire combines components of existing validated instruments with new questions or sections, a careful explanation and justification of its construction must be provided and in particular why overall validity is retained.

A copy of the questionnaire should be included in an appendix.

The chapter should then explain the sampling method used. Many statistical analysis tools assume a simple or stratified random sample. In practice these may be impractical or too expensive (at least for a PhD student) to undertake and many doctoral students resort to pragmatic alternatives such as systematic sampling, cluster sampling, convenience sampling or snowball sampling. These may impose constraints on the subsequent statistical analysis, particularly if the sample size is small (a general rule when using statistical analysis is the smaller the sample size, the greater the scope for subtle problems). A full understanding of these constraints should be demonstrated. If preferred, this discussion can be put in a technical appendix.

The chapter should then explain how the invitation to complete the questionnaire was distributed and how the completed documents (questionnaire and Letter of Informed Consent) were returned. Using current technology, this would most probably be done using a web facilitated questionnaire development and retrieval service. Then the data checking procedures should be described before addressing data analysis. Statistics describing the number of questionnaires returned and the number of usable questionnaires are also necessary. These descriptive statistics should be presented as tables and diagrams such as bar charts.

The name of the software (such as SPSS) used should be stated and any challenges encountered with it should be mentioned.

In the world of quantitative research there are generally accepted ways of presenting your findings and data. If you are not familiar with these, you should read a few papers from good journals which present such research. If you are not well versed in statistical techniques, you should get advice from an experienced statistician. Above all, you should never put into a dissertation any data analysis or statistical measures or techniques that you do not fully understand. To do so is to run the risk of serious trouble in the viva; you might get away with it, but if you are found out it could be disastrous.

Quantitative research tends to produce a large number of reports and in general these should not be included in Chapter 4. A selection of the most important reports needs to be included in an appendix. Sometimes this chapter contains pages and pages repeating the same analysis and statistics for different data sets. This should be avoided. The technique should be explained once in the main body and repetitive detail put (if necessary at all) in the appendices.

This chapter will then reiterate the hypotheses and propositions and will indicate which, if any of them are rejected in the light of the data obtained. This is standard deductive procedure.

Quantitative data may also be used in an exploratory mode using multivariate techniques such as exploratory factor analysis, correspondence analysis, principal component analysis and structured equation modelling. These techniques provide insights which can be used in the process of inductive logic. With this type of analysis hypothesis testing is not conducted. However, it is possible that the theoretical conjecture created by such multivariate techniques could then be tested using hypothesis testing.

As implied above, for a quantitative research project this chapter would end with an overall description of the results of the data analysis and an interpretation of these results leading to an understanding of how the research question may be answered. It should also include an indication as to what extent the researcher regards the research to be replicable and the results to be generalisable.

For qualitative research, when using a case study for example, the different types of evidence obtained need to be listed. This list might contain internal interviews, observations, focus group discussions, corporate documents, financial reports, stockbroker reports, customer or supplier interviews and old press releases to mention only a few sources.

When an interview has been used to collect data the development of the interview schedule needs to be described. In broad terms this process is similar to that required in developing a bespoke questionnaire. However, an interview schedule will probably only have 5 or 6 questions and be designed to facilitate a discussion with the informant over a period of about one hour. Interviews with a small number of questions are commonly referred to as semi-structured and this is the most common type of interview in management research. Interviews can also be structured (which in extreme cases may be little different from a questionnaire) and unstructured. The latter are more common in the early, exploratory stages of a research project.

For structured or semi-structured interviews, a copy of the interview schedule needs to be supplied in the appendix.

The selection of informants, their employers (if different organisations are involved) and their job description, the amount of time spent with each one and the size of the resulting transcript should be presented in this chapter, perhaps in a table.

A rationale for the choice of informants needs to be provided. Often in qualitative research a snowball approach is used, but other approaches (such as interviewing all senior managers or all members of a project team) are quite common.

If a grounded theory approach has been employed, then a theoretical sample will need to have been used and how this was done needs to be explained.

It is seldom appropriate to include the full transcripts in the final dissertation though summary transcripts may need to be included in appendices. It is usual to present a short description (three pages) of each case study in this chapter.

Multiple sources of evidence, such as the observations, corporate documents, and customer interviews mentioned above, need to be fully described. Summaries of these are normally adequate and when the number of summaries are large, as may happen when, say, a large number of documents are examined, some of them may be placed in an appendix.

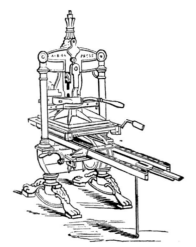

The structure of this chapter will reflect whether the primary purpose of the research is to develop a theory (or extend an existing one) or to test an existing theory. If a qualitative research study is intended to test a theory, then the evidence collected from the different data sources may be used jointly and severally in an attempt to confirm or reject propositions derived from the theory. Testing propositions in qualitative research is less formal than in quantitative research. In qualitative research the data is used to construct an argument by which the propositions are tested. Sometimes the principle of *reductio ad absurdum* is used. The same basic research principle that propositions cannot be proved, but may only be rejected applies to this sort of research.

If the researched question is designed to facilitate the development of a theory, then the data collected from the different sources needs to be integrated into an appropriate synthesis so that a greater understanding of the theoretical implications may be achieved. In this case the data from all the different sources needs to be drawn together into a consistent and convincing argument which can answer the research question. This is driven by an inductive approach and the final output is a theoretical conjecture.

The researcher needs to comment on the research's authenticity, transferability, creditability, dependability and conformability.

The letter or note confirming that ethical approval has been granted should be included in the appendices. Correspondence with the ethics committee may also be included in this appendix as many copies of the letter of informed consent.

This chapter needs to tell the story of how the research was conducted and why the researcher can assert that it has been performed with all due rigour.

The length of this chapter is normally between 30 and 50 pages.

The fifth chapter - Findings and Conclusions

Whereas Chapter 4 describes what was done and this includes reporting the results of the analysis, Chapter 5 addresses what the research findings mean. The philosophical underpinning of this chapter is that unlike the aphorism which states that *"facts speak for themselves"*, researchers believe that facts have to be interpreted with considerable care. There are often multiple possible interpretations of what are presented as indisputable facts. Furthermore, there are facts and facts. Opinions expressed on a five point Likert scale are often presented by positivist researchers as 'hard' data, but they ask users to respond to questions designed by the researcher and to do so by ticking one of only five/seven/nine options. How 'factual' is such data is open to debate. Qualitative data can be even less factual. Problems with memory, priming, reactions to social cues from the interviewer, 20-20 hindsight, an understanding of language and so on mean that interview data should often not be taken at face value. Interpretation is therefore part of the bedrock of the research process. Before discussing this in detail it is important to remember that academic research in business and management studies seeks to deliver both a theoretical contribution as well as insights which can be used by managers and executives engaged in the everyday practice of their professions. Thus this research needs to deliver on both theory and practical advice.

If the research has been theory testing orientated, a series of hypotheses or propositions will have been presented in Chapter(s) 1 and/or 2. Each of these hypotheses or propositions will have been tested against empirical data and where appropriate, hypotheses or propositions will have been accepted or rejected. This will have been described in Chapter 4.

There are three possible outcomes to this type of testing and these are:-

- no evidence has been found to suggest that the theory needs any change or refinement;
- evidence has been found that the theory needs some reformulation;
- evidence suggests that the theory needs to be fully reformulated. In extreme cases, the whole theory may be rejected in a way that is not retrievable.

In general the research will usually be aimed at, in some way, confirming some aspects of the theory being studied. Therefore the researcher will not normally be hoping to reject all of the hypotheses or propositions outright. If this is the outcome, i.e. nothing is rejected, then the researcher simply writes up the finding that the theory remains unchallenged and what the management implications of this are. This can sometimes be problematic in a viva or defence where the examiners might suggest that there is no contribution: all the research has done is prove what is already known. It is therefore important, when simply testing an existing theory, to have a good reason for believing that the theory may be wrong as a basis for justifying the research. The contribution is then to prove that this reason is not valid. You are unlikely to get a PhD for simply replicating somebody else's work and getting the same outcome (see below for more about this).

In the situation where all of the hypotheses are rejected, the researcher is then in a position of being able to discuss why the old theory came into existence and why it survived as long as it did. Then the researcher needs to reformulate a new theory. This is the most creative aspect of the research. Theory generation needs a careful study of the variables involved, how they interact and the possible outcomes. It is obvious that a high degree of creativity and insight may be required here. This outcome rarely happens. Most doctoral research ends up with a revised theory and this is perfectly adequate for a doctorate.

If the results of the hypothesis testing support the rejection of some of the hypotheses then the researcher needs to reformulate the theory in the light of this new knowledge. This reformulation can be a challenge and the researcher will have to engage in some formal theory developing techniques. It is not sufficient to announce that the hypotheses are rejected and leave it there.

Up to this point the researcher has been dealing with academic theory which now needs to be translated into practical concerns.

There is no step-by-step formula for converting theory into management guidelines or management policy directives. Each theory will be specific and its implementation and the consequences thereof will be peculiar to the situation involved. Thus while creating management guidelines is context specific, it is also creative and will require a share of imagination.

The process of taking the results of rejected hypotheses and using these results to modify or fully reformulate a theory is an inductive one. Therefore it is sometimes said that deduction does not often occur on its own, but works hand-in-hand with induction. It should be mentioned that some researchers are suspicious of induction and argue that no matter how much evidence there is supporting a proposition today, there is no guarantee that the same situation leading to this evidence will exist tomorrow. There is an ongoing debate about this proposition, the leading antagonist of which was Karl Popper who strongly argued against the acceptance of knowledge based on induction. Popper pointed out that for thousands of years Europeans were of the belief that a swan was adequately defined as a large white bird. But in 1790 John Latham identified a large black bird in South Western Australia which he later classified as a swan – thus destroying the idea that a swan could be defined as a large white bird. This, Popper argued, demonstrates that no matter how much evidence is collected from which to draw an induction based theory, we can never be sure that there is not an as yet undiscovered exception which will refute our theory. Today we understand that a degree of confidence needs to be associated with any theory formulated as a result of induction and this allows science to operate in terms of an induction based knowledge discovery approach. A researcher would probably benefit from showing that he or she is aware of this matter.

Induction drives theory building research.

Induction takes the data collected and the results of its analysis and uses these to craft a convincing argument which explains what has been happening and formulates that explanation as a theoretical contribution. Although the data may not be exclusively qualitative, induction will often rely extensively on qualitative data with quantitative data playing a supporting role in the interpretation process. This is the most creative aspect of the research and it is not possible to offer a cookbook recipe for the processes involved. Various researchers use different techniques to help their creative thinking processes. Quiet reflection is often helpful. Others use brainstorming or give imaginary lectures to demanding audiences. Some doctoral students use postgraduate seminars to present and test their evolving ideas. One researcher talked about "long walks in the woods" working for him.

Every researcher will discover his or her own individual way of developing a theory and as this is a highly creative process there is only a minimal amount of advice that can be given. In general the first step requires the various issues which have arisen in the transcript to be listed. Then they will have to be ranked in some way which might be in terms of their apparent importance to the informants who have provided the data. Then these are often grouped. One of the analysis techniques sometimes used here is Content Analysis which facilitates counting and sorting of issues and makes a start on ranking them. Some researchers will code the issues in their list. Coding is useful when some summarisation will be done and is essential if this is to be computerised.

When the data is listed, coded, ranked and grouped then a technique called Correspondence Analysis may be used. Correspondence Analysis is a technique developed in France. It is a conceptual mapping tool which is helpful in finding potential relationships between issues. Correspondence Analysis clusters concepts, perceptions, observations and their sources which can help a researcher discover relationships between them. There is a number of other comparable techniques available.

There are other software products which can automate approaches like these and take them further. One of the most popular is N-Vivo which provides a data management facility and the ability to perform extensive cross tabulations. It should be noted that some researchers are critical of computerised approaches arguing that the work involved imports quantitative thinking into qualitative data, i.e. Content Analysis, Correspondence Analysis and cross tabulation all involve counting and as such present a barrier to the real interpretation of the meaning of the data.

None of the techniques described above create theory. They are techniques which can facilitate a creative moment for the researcher. The most they can achieve is to prompt the researcher into seeing relationships between issues and what these relationships might mean. To create a theory the researcher has to take these prompts or suggestions and to formulate them into a theory and put his or her nomenclature on it.

Researchers who wish to distance themselves from these numerically based types of techniques look towards hermeneutic analysis in order to derive an understanding and thus a theory from the data. Hermeneutics is a well established approach for the interpretation and understanding of text. It was first used in the middle of the 19th century to help with the interpretation of biblical text. Before the publishing of Darwin's *Origin of the Species*, the Judeo-Christian holy books were commonly regarded, even in academic circles, as historically accurate and directed by the will of God. However, with the acceptance of evolution the first story of the book of Genesis came to be considered as a metaphor. The result of this was the realisation that there was a need to have a structured way of understanding the rest of the text in the Bible. In modern research, hermeneutics requires the detailed examination of the transcripts acquired from the informants at chapter level (if the material has been organised in that way), at paragraph level and sentence level. It is a technique which draws heavily on detailed intensive reflection on the transcripts created as a result of the data collection activities. The type of reflection required cannot be rushed and this part of theory development can take quite some time.

To be regarded as a hermeneutist it is necessary to learn a specialised language and to follow the rules of that research genre. But like the case of Content and Correspondence Analysis addressed above, hermeneutics is ultimately only capable of offering suggestions to the researcher. The production of the theory is a function of the creativity and imagination of the researcher. Scientific discovery comes from the mind of the researcher. A hermeneutist would argue that theory evolves in the subconscious after deep and lengthy study of the data and reflection on it. There are occasional 'eureka' moments, when a sudden flash of inspiration will strike out of the blue, but inspiration, like chance, favours the prepared mind.

The theory produced by the researcher has to resonate not only with him or herself, but also with the community; the more people who are shown and asked to comment on the new theory the better. An ancient process dating back to Socrates, which is referred to as the dialectic, is helpful. The dialectic requires the new theory voiced by the researcher to be exposed to criticism from other knowledgeable academics (and practitioners) and in this way attempts to refine it through discourse or debate among this group.

There is one more step which a researcher can take in producing a theory. When the researcher is faced with the suggestions and prompts developed from the data, it is often the case that there are several possible interpretations which can be derived from these data. Thus more than one theory could be promulgated. To improve a theory's credibility the researcher should list all the possible rival theories and explain why he or she does not accept any other than the chosen one. This can be a difficult and time consuming process, but it does substantially improve the researcher's case for the acceptance of the chosen theory.

Some researchers will regard the development of a theoretical understanding as an adequate conclusion to their research. The outcome of the theory generation process will be referred to as a new theory or a new theoretical conjecture.

Other researchers go on to create a number of hypotheses or propositions (sometimes the words 'empirical generalisations' are used here) from the theoretical conjecture and test these. This would be done through the process of deductive theory testing described earlier.

Having created a theory, the use of a theory-practice diagram will help the researcher identify areas of business and management practice which the theory will affect. Figure 4 shows a theory-practice impact assessment diagram.

A theory-practice impact assessment diagram is a tool designed to focus the thoughts of a researcher on all of the areas which a new theory might affect. A theory-practice diagram will differ slightly from industry to industry and in some cases new factors will need to be introduced to the diagram or some of the more standard ones may be omitted.

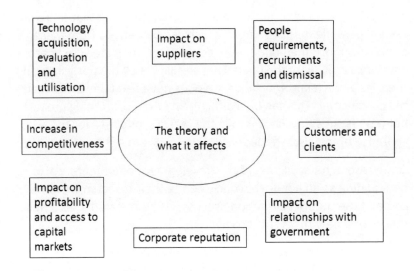

Figure 4: A theory-practice impact assessment diagram

There is no intention of suggesting that the items in the boxes shown in Figure 4 are the only ones which may be affected by a new theory. This figure will need to be modified for each specific situation being researched.

Researchers can draw lines between the theory circle in the model and the different aspects of the business. They can attribute levels of influence which the theory will have on, say for example, relationships with suppliers and/or corporate reputation. This will help the researcher produce some practical guidelines which will be of use to management. But using the diagram will not, on its own, formulate management guidelines or policies. There is no substitute for creative thinking at this stage of the research. Some researchers go as far as saying that here the most important issue in research surfaces and that this is the imagination of the researcher.

This chapter will be between 30 and 50 pages in length.

The final requirement of this chapter is a strong statement that the research has been worthwhile and that it has made a valuable contribution to the body of theoretical knowledge and that it also has important lessons for management. This statement needs to be firm without being pompous or arrogant.

As a final note it is worth mentioning that the process of theory creation described in this section is generic in the sense that it applies to all sorts of qualitative research whether or not GTM is employed or whether a critical theory or other approach is being used.

The sixth chapter - limitations and future research

Whereas in the previous chapters mention has been made of the fact that the researcher needs to reflect on what he or she has been doing and what it means, this chapter is exclusively about the researcher's personal reflections.

The purpose of Chapter 6 is to anticipate criticism from an examiner by identifying any potential limitations in the research and explaining them in advance. The chapter also reports on other interesting questions or phenomena which the researcher has encountered during the research journey and which might be worthy of further research.

It is not the purpose of this chapter to in any way belittle the research which has been done. It is certainly not appropriate for the researcher to suggest that his or her work is incomplete. However, academic research is never perfect. There is nearly always some additional analysis which could have been performed and/or different lenses through which the researcher could have viewed the research question. Larger samples might have been useful. Gaining access to more knowledgeable informants could have improved the results of the research. Studying more cases might have yielded deeper information.

There are always two overarching constraints on any academic research project and these are time and money. Academic research has to be completed within a timeframe which suits the university. The time specified is based on experience and also on the university's own funding arrangements. It is possible that with more time a researcher could have produced more interesting results. Time is always an important consideration as reflecting on the research is critical and forcing reflection into a strict timeframe is known to produce inferior results.

If the researcher had been well enough funded, he or she could have travelled the world to perhaps find more knowledgeable informants. With appropriate funding the researcher could have offered incentives to informants to complete a questionnaire for example or hired a market research firm to execute a proper random sample from the general public. Of course there is a school of thought that suggests that any financial incentive will bias the research findings, but it is not universally believed that the degree of such bias would be a problem. Some journals and consultants' reports are expensive and out of the reach of doctoral candidates unless they have substantial financial backing or their university has a particularly good library.

On a different level, a researcher may have been limited by not having access to all the individuals he or she would have liked during a case study. The organisation may not have been generous enough with making staff or files available. The researcher may not have been allowed access to certain documents. Some aspects of the topic being studied may be considered confidential by the organisation. Ethical considerations may also preclude some questions being asked or even some people being interviewed. Although an organisation may allow a researcher in, they can impose severe limitations on what he or she can realistically find out.

Some of the documents may have been in another language and this may have reduced the researcher's ability to extract data from them.

The researcher's ability to use a statistical package (or his or her knowledge of statistical methods) may not have been as complete as he or she may have wished. This would not necessarily have produced a fatal flaw in the work, but it could have led to limitations.

Some researchers find it difficult to articulate the limitations of their research. This comes from being so immersed in the research project for a substantial number of years. What is needed here is a way of moving from the current working mode which focuses on getting things done to a more reflective mode of standing back from the action requirements of everyday work. There is a technique which a researcher may use to assist with the reflection which is required in this chapter. Good research practice recommends that a research log or a research diary be kept throughout the period of the project. This diary should not only record events and meetings, but it should be used to note new insights which the researcher acquired during the project. This offers excellent input to the reflection process. In addition to the diary the researcher can create, from the entries therein, a research concept audit trail. The idea of the audit trail has been borrowed from the accounting profession which requires the detail of financial transactions to be traceable. The idea of a research concept audit trail is to be able to trace the cognitive development of the research during the final process of reflection on the work performed for the research project.

Academic research is always a voyage of discovery. By this is meant, amongst other things, that it is hard to be certain about the value of the research question, the appropriateness of the methodology or the utility of the research findings, in advance of the research being performed. It is therefore often the case that during the research process it transpires that there are even more interesting questions which could have been explored which the researcher is unable to address because of the need to complete his or her work within a given time and given budget. There may also be innovative methodologies which the researcher discovers and which again may present opportunities to understand the research question in a different light.

There is another dimension to the matter of future research which relates to the principal risk factor involved in academic research. Undertaking a research degree is a substantial task requiring a large investment in time and in funding. Most researchers do not want to take on any larger risks than they have to with regard to the subject they research and how they research it as they want to be as certain as they possibly can be of a successful outcome. Once a degree has been obtained, and this applies especially to doctoral research, the researcher can take on more challenging and more risky research projects. It is these future research challenges which the researcher should report in the final chapter. These suggestions are for areas which the researcher may wish to pursue personally or they may be research opportunities or ideas which others might like to take up.

From the point of view of the examiners, this last section of the dissertation provides some insight into how the researcher's thinking has matured and developed over the period of the research. It should show that the researcher has acquired the ability to be able to see really good or interesting research opportunities and this is one of the signs of a mature researcher.

This chapter is likely to be between 15 and 25 pages in length.

Of course, this is not an opportunity for the researcher to list a number of suggestions for impossible research projects which are completely unreasonable.

Part 4 – The dissertation as a whole and integrated document

A doctoral dissertation is likely to be between 250 and 400 pages in length. The word count equivalent of this in many universities is approximately 80,000. As parsimony is a basic principle of academic research, examiners are generally not impressed by researchers who take more words than this to report their work.

The dissertation should be presented as a single volume book. It will typically have 6 or 7 chapters. In general there should be only one chapter on the literature review and one on the research methodology, although examiners may be prepared to accept two chapters on either or both of these areas. Implied in the specification of the approximate number of pages per chapter suggested in this book is the notion of balance within the dissertation. It would not be acceptable to find the chapter on methodology constituting half of the dissertation, for example.

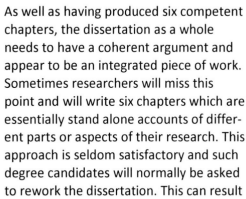

As well as having produced six competent chapters, the dissertation as a whole needs to have a coherent argument and appear to be an integrated piece of work. Sometimes researchers will miss this point and will write six chapters which are essentially stand alone accounts of different parts or aspects of their research. This approach is seldom satisfactory and such degree candidates will normally be asked to rework the dissertation. This can result in a considerable amount of additional work.

What needs to be remembered at all times is that the dissertation is an account of the research from its inception in the mind of the researcher to the delivery of results which can be said to constitute a valuable contribution to the body of knowledge presented with a high degree of scholarship.

The dissertation needs to be professionally finished and to achieve this, its physical presentation is important. The dissertation should be bound in keeping with the rules of the university. Most universities do not require hard cover binding until the dissertation has been examined and all the required changes have been made and approved. The university will often have rules about the colour of the binding and the finish of the text on the cover.

As mentioned above, sometimes single sided printing is required. Some universities still require the work to be printed doubled spaced. Paper of a particular weight e.g. 80 gsm is sometimes specified. If heavy paper is used, then the dissertation will appear to be bigger than it would otherwise.

Similarly if the dissertation is too long, thinner paper can be used to disguise this. Such tactics should be avoided.

Increasingly an electronic copy of the dissertation is required to be submitted. This may be processed through a plagiarism testing software tool of which there are several available on the web. Researchers should be aware that plagiarism testing software tools will usually find any direct quotations which have been used in the document and this will be reported. As mentioned elsewhere in this book, a certain amount of direct referencing is acceptable if not actually desirable.

It is important to establish how many copies need to be presented for examination and then for final acceptance. It is common to have to produce five copies for examination. This would be one for each examiner and one for each of the supervisors as well as one for the chairperson of the viva voce. When the work is finally completed there are usually three copies required: one for the Director of Research's Office, one for the library and one for the supervisor. Of course the graduate often makes more copies than this.

Part 5 – Some General Thoughts

From the point of view of writing the dissertation or thesis there are 10 important rules which have to be followed:

- Start writing early.
- Use writing to clarify your thoughts.
- Write definitions and descriptions of concepts when you encounter them and refine them as you proceed.
- Collect diagrams in appropriately named files which you can use when you come to the final write up.
- Find out what referencing system you need to comply with and use it from day one.
- Make sure that references are recorded down to the detail of page number where appropriate from the beginning.
- Make the acquisition of writing skills a priority.
- Organise yourself in a writing group or get yourself on a writing course if you have any doubt about your writing skills.
- Make sure that you feed your written work to your supervisor steadily and a little at a time.
- Make sure that you have your work thoroughly proofread before submission.

Part 6 – The leading pages

Cover page

Each university has specific rules as to the information which is re-quired on the cover of a dissertation.

As a minimum this will include:-

- Name of degree candidate;
- The title of the dissertation or thesis;
- The name of the university;
- The name of the faculty, department or school;
- The date of submission;
- The name of the supervisor.

Some of the detail described above for the cover page, which is the first page in the dissertation, is normally repeated on the actual book cover itself. There will typically be rules specifying what is re-quired on the cover. Some universities have a preferred outside binding organisation which knows the rules for binding dissertations and it is useful to ascertain if this is the case and if so, to use this service.

There are rules as regards the title of the dissertation. Universities normally ask for the title to be contained to a maximum number of words. The number does vary, but it is usually in the 12 to 20 word range. What is certainly discouraged is paragraph length titles. A sub-title containing a few more words is normally allowed in addition to the main title.

Abstract

An abstract is a short summary of the dissertation or thesis. The abstract should be written using a positive tone encouraging a prospective reader to explore the dissertation. The abstract should state the research question and why it is important, what methodology was used in the research, the findings and the conclusions. Abstracts should be short. It is preferable if the abstract is held to one page but two pages should be considered a maximum.

Certificates of own work

Universities will ask for one or more declarations to be included in the dissertation certifying that the researcher has:

- Conducted the research him or herself;
- Not submitted the research to any other university for any other degree or diploma;
- Readiness to be included in the library;
- Other certificates may also be required.

Sometimes all the certification is included in one certificate which is then signed by the degree candidate.

In rare cases a dissertation may contain confidential commercial or other information which precludes its being put in the library for general availability. This is usually referred to as putting an embargo (or sometimes a stay) on the dissertation. A reader may have to get permission to access the work. Some academics and universities do not like this, arguing that both academic freedom and the fact that the university is publicly funded requires that complete work should be in the public domain for other scholars and researchers to build on. Such a restriction may also prevent the researcher from publishing his or her work in academic journals – an important part of building his or her career and CV. On the other hand, such a policy can prevent some types of research from ever being done. Should the question of restricted publication be raised, this should be discussed with the university and supervisor and any implications should be fully understood before starting on the research.

Acknowledgement

Researchers will receive support from a number of different individuals. There will be at a minimum his or her supervisor/s. There could be help from family or from friends. Other members of faculty may have spent time talking over various aspects of the research protocol. Whatever help has been received should be acknowledged.

Dedication (if any)

Some researchers wish to acknowledge the importance of an individual or a number of individuals in their life by dedicating their work thereto. Not every dissertation will have a dedication.

Other academic outputs

If the researcher has delivered seminars on this research to faculty or to student groups in the university this should be mentioned here. Some researchers will have been invited to present at other universities and institutions and this should also be recorded.

If the researcher had delivered one or more papers on this research at a conference or had a paper or papers published in a journal then it is important to note it here. Sometimes doctoral researchers have two or three peer reviewed papers published from their work before they submit their dissertation. This can considerably strengthen the researcher's position in a viva, especially if publication has been in a top journal.

Table of contents

While a detailed table of contents is required it should not include too many subsections of paragraphs. The table of contents should not run into tens of pages.

Tables of figures and tables of tables

It is helpful to have a list of the figures and tables employed in the dissertation.

Appendices

The appendices will normally include the following.

List of references

The list of references used should contain entries for all sources of authority cited in the dissertation. There are several different standards for references. The most frequently used in business and management studies is the Harvard Referencing System (MHRA Style Guide 2009). This system is also called the Name Date System or the In-text Citation System.

The researcher needs to ascertain the university's requirements and learn how to reference competently. The manner in which the references are used should be flawless.

Some universities and academics use the term bibliography instead of reference list. The term bibliography is sometimes used to create a list of all the relevant published and unpublished sources which the researcher has encountered during his or her research or of general readings on the topic. Such a list would include papers, books etc., which were not cited in the work. This is not required in a list of references.

In a dissertation in which 200 or 300 references are cited it is easy for mistakes to be made in the list of references and thus this part of the dissertation should be carefully checked before the final submission of the work.

Glossary

Specialised terms will often be used in a dissertation and such terms need defining. But do not include terms which will be commonly known to readers in this field. As mentioned earlier in this text, when definition of terms was discussed, it is inappropriate to repeat definitions found in dictionaries or encyclopaedias to create the glossary. The researcher needs to consult peer reviewed journals and also contribute his or her own thinking to the explanation of the terms in the glossary.

Abbreviations and/or acronyms used

Most substantial pieces of work will employ numerous abbreviations and/or acronyms. These should be available to the reader in an easily accessible table. Apart from being in the appendices, acronyms and abbreviations should always be explained the first time they are used in the body of the dissertation. If they have not been used for a while (say 30 or more pages), there is no harm in explaining them again.

Some dissertations place the list of acronyms and abbreviations at the front of the work.

Questionnaire or interview schedule/s

It is necessary to supply all the relevant documentation which was employed during the research process. However, it is generally felt that the flow of the argument created in each chapter should not be disrupted by the reader being presented with lengthy questionnaires or interview schedules. These may be included in an appendix.

Research protocol

The research protocol, which is a detailed plan of how the research was to be conducted and which is often created as part of a research proposal, should be included in the final dissertation as an appendix.

Ethics protocol and related correspondence

An application for the approval of the research by the ethics committee will have been sought and obtained. This will require a form to be completed and presented to the ethics committee. This normally results in some correspondence before final approval is acquired by the researcher.

All the correspondence entered into as well as the final letter of approval should be included in this section.

Where ethical approval is required from and provided by an outside body (such as a school or hospital board) this too should be included here.

Data acquired - either transcripts or numeric tables

Qualitative data results in transcripts of interviews or descriptions of observations or extracts from reports or other documents and often consists of large volumes of data. It is necessary to present some summaries from these sources. The nature and size of the summaries will depend on the research question. The summaries are required to give the examiners a clear indication of the analysis and the synthesis which the researcher undertook.

Quantitative data will result in numerous statistical type reports and a number of the more important of these reports should be included in an appendix. The topic and the nature of the research question will determine which reports to include. It is not normally the case that the actual data collected will be included in the dissertation.

Care needs to be taken to use the data reports judiciously so that they support the argument in the dissertation without overwhelming the work and producing an excessively large book.

Other detailed explanatory evidence acquired

There may be other important sources of evidence to which the researcher wants to draw the attention of the examiners such as photographs, certificates or copies of correspondence. These should be included in an appendix.

Part 7 – Data Management: Makes writing up much easier

Although this is seldom if ever offered as advice, one of the first activities academic researchers should undertake is the acquisition of a substantial filing cabinet. And due to the fact that ethics committees today require assurances that all data obtained by the researcher will be held securely, it is important that the filing cabinet has a lock and key.

With very few exceptions, academic research projects accumulate substantial amounts of data. The data will mainly be in the form of field notes, transcripts of interviews and focus groups, completed questionnaires, published reports, press clippings, as well as photographs and video and audio recordings.

Creating a filing system whereby the data collected by the researcher can be easily retrieved is fundamental to sound research practice. This involves the acquisition of a number of physical files in which papers collected by the researcher can be systematically stored. Some of this data may well be eventually digitised and stored on computer but there will always be the need to secure the original source documents.

Much of what can be said about data management for academics will be regarded by many researchers to be common sense. However, it is a well known fact that common sense is not all that common and thus it is worth while using a few pages to point out some of the issues and making a few suggestions. Effective data management planning can prevent a number of problems occurring and facilitate an early completion of the research.

Data management may be defined in this context as putting in place procedures and practices which will prevent data loss from delaying or disrupting a research project. Of course it is not sufficient to define or simply specify these procedures and practices. They have to be conscientiously followed and this is quite difficult for many researchers. Despite the tedium involved, taking care of your work is of prime importance. Even if you back up regularly to an offsite location, a data loss the one time that you forget to do it can cause you a lot of grief – especially if it happens when you are close to submission and under pressure from deadlines.

In the production of a research dissertation a large amount of writing is necessary. In addition there will often be numerous graphs and diagrams as well as other figures and tables generated by software packages. Preparation of a dissertation will normally involve a word processor, a spreadsheet and possibly other presentation software not to mention statistical packages such as SPSS or analysis tools such as nVivo. Some doctorates may have sufficient data to justify using a relational or other structured database. Microsoft has by far the leading position in the market for office software and thus the most likely systems will be Word, Excel and PowerPoint. It is beyond the scope of this book to address specific issues related to these products but nonetheless it may be helpful to consider some of the data or file management issues associated with a large research project when using these tools.

Directory and file names

How documents are filed in the computer can make the researcher's work relatively easy or it can lead to confusion and the need for rework. Without proper file management documents can be lost or can be inappropriately deleted. Any reworking is wasteful and should be wherever possible avoided. The first issue here is that an easy-to-use directory and file naming system is required. The second issue is that it is essential to create and maintain a backup regime throughout the research project. Devising the correct structure on day one can save you many hours of work later, so this deserves a bit of thought before you set it up.

Directories and subdirectories

The first step is to create and name a master directory for all the files related to the research project on the disk of your principal computer. Within this directory there will be the need for a number of subdirectories. The number and the content of these subdirectories will depend to a considerable extent on the type of research being undertaken. It will also depend on the data management style of the researcher. Planning the layout of these directories can be very helpful to the smooth operation and this plan could be seen as a road map to the data required for the dissertation write-up.

If empirical research is being conducted it will often be useful to have a subdirectory for the data collected and a separate subdirectory for the writing up. If different types of data are involved a researcher might wish to have one subdirectory for quantitative data which might be in Excel files and another subdirectory for qualitative data, which could be in Word files. Depending upon the software used to analyse the data, more files of different types will be created and it may be appropriate to store these in different directories. As a general rule do not nest directories more than two or three times as deeply nested directories can cause data to be forgotten or mislaid.

Within the writing up subdirectory some researchers like to create another level of subdirectories, one for each chapter in the dissertation and one each for the appendices and the references (if the latter are not stored in something like EndNote). This can be useful as there will no doubt be a number of different versions of the text for each chapter and a large number of files can be confusing. It is important to incorporate a version indicator - usually a number in the file title. It is hard to over-emphasise the importance of version control. Losing track of which version is current can be frustrating and can waste a lot of valuable time. In a worst case scenario it can lead to errors in the dissertation.

On the question of version control another problem which may arise is having to deal with many old versions of the same file. Good practice with computer housekeeping requires old versions of files to be deleted when new versions are in use and have been backed up correctly.

There is an art in file and directory naming. Try to design something simple, meaningful and flexible. Do not set up too many directories; keep it manageable.

Merging files or combining data

As the write-up develops there may be the need to merge files with text and files with data such as tables, diagrams or graphs. On this account it is important to be aware of the size of the resulting file. The file size can grow surprisingly large and not all computers (or mail systems) operate well with large files although this is a diminishing problem. There are techniques for controlling the size of files and researchers should become familiar with these. Particular attention should be given to image files as the file type and resolution will affect both the appearance and the size of the resulting file. Furthermore, if images are copied into a text file and then cropped, it is a good idea to then cut them from the text file and paste them back so as to lose the cropped data from the file.

As the file size grows the researcher should take more care with regular saving and backing up procedures as there is obviously more to lose.

Backing up data

Many researchers will lose some data at some time during the research project. The loss of data is painful and may actually put the whole research project in jeopardy. Researchers who do not make adequate arrangements for backing up are effectively gambling with this project.

As a general rule you should back up every day during periods of moderate activity and several times a day during periods of intense writing and/or analysis. Many universities provide an automated backup service and you can use this if it is available, but during highly active periods it may not be frequent enough. If not, you should have your own backup to a reliable medium which is kept offsite in a safe location. The minimum number of backups is one, but two is advisable. This is often referred to as a 'father and grandfather' system whereby you overwrite the day before yesterday's 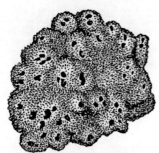 backup with today's backup. Where files are not too big, a simple and effective form of backup is to e-mail the files to a friend and ask them to keep the copy in their mail system. You can also mail the backups to yourself though if your file sizes are large, you will need to pay attention to your assigned mailbox space.

Be careful in your choice of backup media. Traditionally most researchers use a secondary storage unit directly under their control with which to back up their data. Until relatively recently, this might have been a CD or a DVD or some sort of fast tape machine. Increasingly, memory sticks also known as flash drives are now being used for this purpose. Although excellent in many respects, these memory sticks are vulnerable especially to loss, theft (and failure). To overcome this, researchers sometimes keep a number of copies of their data and write-up and this can in turn lead to version identification problems (see below). If you have a particularly large volume of data it may be worth buying a small portable hard disk drive. These are inexpensive and robust.

Another approach to backing up is to use cloud based services supplied by a number of major companies globally. If you do this, the backing up process can be looked after by the outsourcer and your data will be stored in various parts of the world. On the face of it this arrangement appears to offer many advantages and can offer peace of mind to the researcher. However, many countries have data protection legislation and this can proscribe that certain types of data cannot be transmitted across national borders of certain countries. Bear in mind too that while some cloud providers offer quite low cost options for moderate amounts of data storage, costs can rise steeply if you go over a certain threshold. It is not likely that many dissertations will do this, but check the fine print before signing any agreement with a cloud supplier.

Whatever approach is taken to backing up it is important to test its effectiveness from time to time. Computers are not infallible and data can be corrupted. The researcher should be reasonably confident that the data can be restored in a useful way.

Finally as regards backing up, because computer technology now plays such an important role in research it is often forgotten that taking a paper copy of data and partial write-ups is also a backup – perhaps the backup of the last resort.

Reference management software

Another strand of data which needs planning and control is the recording of detailed references used in the dissertation. Irrespective of whether or not empirical research is being undertaken, the researcher will be required to demonstrate that a large number of the published works of others has been read and understood. This reading needs to be recorded in a reference list and there are today a number of specialised products which can assist with this task. End-Note is one of the best known. However the reference list may also be created in a word processor such as Word or any other database type product.

Summary and conclusion

Like so many other issues in research, with a little data management and contingency planning many tedious problems can be avoided.

The first step is to create a road map of how the different types of files will be stored on a directory by directory basis.

The second step is to create a standard for file naming with a strong emphasis on the fact that many files will have multiple versions.

The third step is to be aware of the implications of large files.

The last step is to decide your backup policy and ensure that these back up arrangements are satisfactory and in particular that they will work if and when they are needed.

Part 8 – The Monograph Dissertation versus the Papers Approach

Some universities offer a number of different routes to a doctorate. The approach discussed in this book is described as gaining a doctorate by completing a material research project under supervision[1]. At the conclusion of this process the candidate must demonstrate clearly that he or she has added something of value to the body of theoretical knowledge and has some ability to improve practice as well as that the research has been conducted to a high standard of scholarship.

QUARTER-STAFF.

There are different ways in which these objectives may be realized. The two most significant are the Monograph Disserta-

---

[1] Some universities are now allowing work which was not conducted by the research degree candidate under supervision to be included in their doctoral dissertations. This could be papers written and published before the candidate considered registering for a doctorate. The term Professional PhD has been coined by some universities and business schools to denote such a degree.

tion and the Papers Approach[2]. Most universities offer both of these routes, although the Monograph Dissertation route is by far the best known and is thus regarded by some academics to be the less risky. This chapter compares these two approaches and considers their relative advantages and disadvantages.

The Monograph Dissertation

In a Monograph Dissertation the research is reported in one book, by one author[3] and the completed work is of substantial length. The work is examined as a single entity only when it is complete. The structure of the Monograph Dissertation has been described in preceding chapters. Most dissertations completed in universities today are produced in this way; although there is currently an upturn in interest in the Papers Approach to doctorates, many academics are not even aware of this method.

Papers Approach

The Papers Approach to doctoral research requires the research degree candidate to undertake a number of separate, but related pieces of research which will be written up and 'published' individually as well as being included in the final dissertation. Universities normally require three such publications, although there are some institutions which demand four or even five. The different pieces of research need to address a common research problem and they have to display a high degree of coherence. The papers included may thus be seen as a portfolio of work. In addition to this portfolio,

---

[2] The Paper Approach is also called the Article Approach. The term paper is more academically formal than article.

[3] In certain parts of the world universities allow research degrees to be undertaken jointly by multiple individuals and who may produce only one dissertation. Some academics believe that this is against the spirit of doctoral research.

most universities which allow this method also require from the candidate two accompanying narratives. These two narratives are bound together with the papers into one book. The first narrative introduces the research problem, discusses some aspects of the literature and comments on the methodological issues involved. This narrative will also cover any ethics issues in the research. The second narrative presents a summary and conclusion as well as a discussion of the limitations of the work and suggestions for further research.

Do the Papers need to be published?

The Papers need to be 'published' or near 'published'. Originally this route to the doctorate required the Papers to be published in peer reviewed journals[4]. However, it soon became apparent that waiting for the appearance of the papers in print took too much time. Peer reviewed journals can take several years to process a paper before it finally appears in print. As a result of such delays universities began to allow papers to be included in the portfolio of the research degree candidate's work which had only been accepted by a journal for publication. In some universities papers which have only been submitted, but not yet reviewed, are deemed acceptable. However, it is always better for the credibility of the research if the papers have been published in a respected, peer reviewed academic journal.

In general, the submission of a paper to a peer reviewed academic journal is the minimum, although papers that have been internally reviewed or submitted and accepted by a working paper series are sometimes accepted. Internally reviewed papers need to be as-

---

[4] The university will have a list of acceptable journals and the papers submitted for the Papers Approach to the dissertation will normally need to have been accepted for publication by one of these journals.

sessed by competent internal reviewers (senior members of the school, perhaps) and confirmed to be of a 'publishable' standard.

Some universities require these papers to be written by the research degree candidate alone i.e. as a single authored paper[5]. Others allow co-authored papers to be included in the portfolio. When a co-authored paper is used the university normally requires a certificate from the co-author/s to the effect that the majority of the work conducted and reported in the paper was undertaken by the research degree candidate. Even where such a certificate is provided, examiners may not be entirely comfortable with such papers. A particular case of joint author is the supervisor. It is not unusual to find the supervisor's name as a co-author on these papers. Where co-authored papers are allowed it is sometimes required by the university that at least one solely published paper is included in the portfolio.

If some of all of the papers in the portfolio are as yet unpublished, they will have to comply with the style requirements of the journal to which they will eventually be sent. They also need to comply with the maximum length of paper which the journal will accept. This is typically in the region of 8,000 words. This can lead to a dissertation being formatted in different typefaces or with different referencing conventions. The two narratives may be in yet another style mandated by the university. As with the monograph, it is important to be clear on the university's rules with regard to formatting.

The research topic and the individual research

Having set out these two different routes to a doctorate it is important to be aware that it may be more appropriate to address some

---

[5] It would be unusual if there were no single authored papers in the portfolio of research work.

research topics through the Monograph Dissertation rather than the Papers Approach. In the wrong circumstances, the Papers Approach can result in three separate pieces of research with three data sets, three different collection exercises, three different methodologies and three different structures. Some researchers will find the Monograph Dissertation more congenial to their mind set than the Papers Approach and, of course, vice versa. Besides the question of the suitability of the research topic and the researcher's own orientation there is the question of whether there is a suitable supervisor available who feels competent in assisting the researcher with the Papers Approach. There are not many such supervisors available.

A rushed decision as to which approach to take, may well lead to a number of problems later.

Leading and Ending Narratives

The Leading and the Ending Narratives are material pieces of work and may constitute a considerable amount of the effort required to obtain the degree, especially if the candidate is drawing on his or her existing portfolio[6] for the papers. When the Leading and the Ending Narratives and the three to five papers are bound for presentation for examination, they may constitute nearly as many pages as a Monograph Dissertation on the same research topic.

The Leading Narrative

The Leading Narrative effectively takes the place of the first three chapters of the traditional Monograph Dissertation. This narrative explains what the research problem is and why it is important. Like

---

[6] In theory all the research presented for a doctorate should have been conducted under supervision. However sometimes universities allow some parts of the final portfolio of the researcher to have predated the research degree candidates registration.

the Introductory Chapter in the Monograph Dissertation it will also state how the research has been divided among the number of papers required. The title of each of these papers and a two or three sentence description of the paper needs to be supplied. Then the literature has to be reviewed and the methodology or methodologies used have to be discussed together with the ethical considerations[7]. Examples of Letters of Consent and applications for an ethics protocol and other such documents can be supplied in the Appendices. There will inevitably be some overlap between what is said in this narrative and what will also need to be discussed in the individual papers as any publishable academic papers needs to address these issues in their own right. In the interest of parsimony overlap needs to be kept to a minimum, although in these circumstances some degree of overlap will perhaps be inevitable.

The Ending Narrative

The Ending Narrative draws together the research results described in the individual papers and argues that they may be considered as a cohesive body of research. This involves discussing the conclusions and the application of the results to practice. Limitations and future research challenges are also discussed here.

It is in this section that the research degree candidate needs to argue that the research has made a contribution to the body of theoretical knowledge and that it has application for professional or other performance in practical situations. In addition, it is here that the researcher argues for the authority on which the research is based and this includes the validity, reliability and the generalisability issues.

---

[7] With this approach issues such as ethical consideration may well be duplicated.

This section of the work is of critical importance as the research has to integrate the Leading Narrative and the published papers into a convincing argument and many researchers find this a daunting challenge.

Why undertake a Papers Approach to the Dissertation?

The Paper Approach to the dissertation is sometimes incorrectly believed to be intrinsically less demanding than the Monograph Dissertation. This is seldom if ever the case. The three/four/five papers have to be assessed and are subject to examiners demanding changes. Then the final dissertation is subject to examination and different examiners may require further changes to be made to the work[8]. The length of the Papers Approach Dissertation may be in some cases a little shorter than the Monograph Dissertation but this need not necessarily be the case.

Probably the main motivation for taking the Papers Approach is that Monograph Dissertations are seldom read by anyone other than the degree examiners. Published papers are the recognised means of communicating the results of research to the academic community and therefore the work undertaken for the degree will have a much higher probability of being seen and cited by other academics. For research degree candidates who wish to follow an academic career these publications may be a fast track route to finding a suitable academic post. Of course many, if not most, new doctors will seek

---

[8] Of course with the Paper Approach a dissertation examiner cannot call for changes to be made to the papers if they are already published or even if they have simply been accepted for publication. One of the interesting challenges the research degree candidate faces as a result of the papers being published is that if the papers have been published in different journals there may well have been quite different advice offered by different reviewers and this would be reflected in papers themselves.

to publish a number of papers out of their monograph dissertation research. The how of this is beyond this book, but it is normally possible to publish at least one paper and as many as three and four papers if the research is suitable.

Which route to the doctorate should be preferred?

Like so many questions which are asked concerning doctoral studies there is no simple answer to whether a researcher should take the Monograph Dissertation or the Papers Approach. Both are acceptable routes and both can lead to the two requirements which need to be present for a doctoral degree to be awarded.

The Papers Approach is not at this time a popular route to a doctorate degree. This means that not many supervisors have experience of supporting a research degree candidate in obtaining a degree this way. Similarly there is not much experience in the university system in respect to the examination of these degrees. Academics who are unfamiliar with this approach to doctoral studies have raised concerns about some of the research being published in advance of the submission of the final dissertation. They have suggested that the appearance of such papers in journals could be construed as making their inclusion in the dissertation a form of self plagiarism. It has also been said that if the work has been previously published then it cannot be regarded as original. Fortunately these are minority views.

The Papers Approach to doctoral studies should not be undertaken lightly and certainly not as an 'easy' option. Both the research degree candidate and the supervisor need to be in agreement as to how this work will be conducted and how examiners sympathetic to this route will be found.

With regard to the examination of a doctorate produced by the Papers Approach it is important to bear in mind that some academics may not feel competent to examine such a document and thus care needs to be taken with the appointment of examiners.

On the other hand it has been argued that the Paper Approach should, in time, become popular with examiners because if the final dissertation contains papers that have already been reviewed then the examiners may be inclined to think that the research need not be scrutinized in quite as rigorous a manner as would have been necessary if there had been no former review of the work.

Writing of the Paper

The writing of a paper has some similarities to the writing of a dissertation although there are a number of important differences. Although the format of academic papers often follows that of a dissertation there is the important issue of the maximum number of words. As mentioned above journals will normally limit submission to a maximum of 8,000 words and this can be problematic when attempting to report a significant piece of research. Nonetheless journals are frequently uncompromising about this issue. It is also important that researchers learn the principles of parsimonious writing in order to be able to produce comprehensive and competent work of an appropriately defined length.

Furthermore not all academic papers will follow the same outline of a dissertation and the relative importance of the sections in a paper as opposed to a dissertation may vary considerably. Any research degree candidate wishing to obtain a degree using the Papers Approach will need to be become familiar with the different requirements for an academic paper.

As mentioned above, it is also of central importance that the researcher complies with all the style issues which the journal requires. These will be supplied by the journal and the researcher needs to bear them in mind from the outset of the writing process.

Part 9 - Authors' reflections on the contents of this book

Over the years we have helped a number of research degree candidates obtain their masters or doctoral degrees and what this book represents is a recounting of the issues we have encountered on which they have needed advice and help and how the challenges they faced were solved.

However, a research degree is essentially a creative event and as such the research degree candidate should not need to be told how to do the research nor should he or she be told how to write it up. Supervisors are advisors and not instructors. This does not suit everyone and it is one of the causes of the low completion rates found in some universities and some faculties.

Our intention with this book is to provide a candle to the research degree candidate while he or she finds their own electric switch. The type of thinking required to obtain a research degree cannot be taught in the normal sense of the word 'taught'. A research degree is essentially a self development opportunity and this is not always made explicitly clear to degree candidates. But even when the university is remiss in this regard, sooner or later in the research process, this becomes clear.

This is especially true when it comes to helping someone learn how to write appropriately at a senior academic degree level. As has been pointed out already in this book, writing is primarily a craft skill or maybe even an art and if it does not come naturally to a researcher then the only course of action is to learn these skills while working alongside an accomplished practitioner. This is always a slow process and sometimes it is a painful one as well.

The level of detail at which examiners read a dissertation is some-times surprising to degree candidates and they often have difficulty in accepting what this means. Every word in the dissertation will be read and examiners will ask why a particular word is the most ap-propriate to use in the context in which it is being read. At the ex-amination of this document there is no question of a high level un-derstanding of the material being adequate. It is detail that counts here. Bear in mind that examiners are generally top class academics and have achieved this status by, inter alia, a deeply critical ap-proach to research and thinking.

As mentioned before from time to time, we have been asked if a researcher may use a completely different format (order of chapters and even content of chapters) than the one described in this book. A researcher once suggested that he would prefer to deliver the results in the first chapter, then the methodology and then the lit-erature review and so forth. In the spirit of creativity, which is an essential part of obtaining a research degree, we cannot say that idiosyncratic formats in a dissertation will not be accepted. The final decision will be with the board of examiners, having due regard for the examiners' reports. What we can say is that we have described the current practice with regard to dissertation layout and that to the best of our knowledge this is what the majority of examiners will require.

The responsibility for the production and the defence of a research degree candidate's dissertation during the viva voce is entirely in the hands of the degree candidate and this is both a great challenge and a great opportunity for the researcher.

We wish all our readers success in obtaining their degree.

Appendix 1 – Reference list

MHRA Style Guide,2009, 2nd Ed., Modern Humanities Research Association, London

Remenyi D and A Money (2012), Research Supervision for Supervisors and their Students, Academic Publishing, Reading, UK

Sutton R and B Staw, (1995), What Theory is Not, ASQ, 40, September, p371-384

Webster J and R Watson, (2002), Analyzing the past to prepare for the future: Writing a literature review, MIS Quarterly Vol. 26 No. 2, pp. xiii-xxiii/June

Weick K, (1995), What Theory is Not, Theorizing Is, ASQ, September, p385-390

Whetten D, (1989) , What Constitutes a Theoretical Contribution? Academy of Management Review,, Vol. 14, No. 4, 490-495

Wittgenstein, L. (1969), On Certainty (Uber Gewissheit), sct. 378 (ed. by G Anscombe and G von Wright,) Basil Blackwell, Oxford

Appendix 2 – Interesting websites

http://www.youtube.com/watch?v=LUsb9vf8Lww&feature=fvsr

http://www.youtube.com/watch?v=WRnVdN3NhWc&feature=related

http://www.writers-block-help.com/

http://www.writersandartists.co.uk/

http://www.rjgeib.com/thoughts/steinbeck/steinbeck.html

http://www.youtube.com/watch?v=iobYihZ4FvQ&feature=related

http://www.dissertation-help.co.uk/dissertation_guide/dissertation.htm

http://www.methodspace.com/

http://www.associationofbusinessschools.org/

http://www.mywritinglab.com/

http://www.grammarcheck.net/

http://www.spellchecker.net/grammar/

http://www.doaj.org/

http://grammar.about.com/od/terms/Glossary_of_Grammatical_Rhetoric al_Terms.htm

http://grammartips.homestead.com/quotationmarks.html

Appendix 3 – Number of pages in a typical doctoral dissertation

Although each university has individual in-house rules that cover the general content and structure of a dissertation the following guidelines may be helpful for research degree candidates. The supervisor should ensure that all students are aware of these from quite early in the research process.

Chapter 0	Acknowledgements, dedication, certificate of 'own work', abstract, etc	10 pages
Chapter 1	Why this research is important and to whom it is important	10-20 pages
Chapter 2	Concepts, theories and frameworks leading to a model and research question (= a critical literature review)	30-40 pages
Chapter 3	Methodology, research design, data/ evidence, gathering alternatives, possible analytical strategies (Show comprehensive knowledge of a number of alternatives)	40-50 pages
Chapter 4	The research (The story of the research, created questionnaire, sent to, validated by them etc., or conducted case studies or in-depth interviews or action research etc.)	30-50 pages
Chapter 5	Findings, interpretation, discussion and conclusions and guidelines created (What did we learn from the research and what does it mean?)	40-50 pages
Chapter 6	Limitations of the research. Suggestions for future research (How would you go about this if you were to start again?)	10 pages
Reading list	Approximately 200 references mainly from refereed journals	
Appendices	Questionnaires + interview summaries + URLs + Glossary etc	50–100 pages

= Total of between 250 – 300 bound pages

Appendix 4 – Some common errors to avoid when writing

There are many guides on how to write good English and a detailed exposition on this is beyond the scope of this book. However there are several common errors of commission and omission in English which are found in academic writing. These are simple things to avoid. The following list is not exhaustive, but covers a number of the more common problems.

Using the first person singular ('I') or plural ('we'). As a general rule, the first person singular should be avoided unless you are describing something that you have done and can only do so in a way that would be awkward to say otherwise. There will normally be very few cases in a research degree where it will be appropriate to use the first person plural.

Referring to yourself in the third person (e.g. 'the author' or 'the researcher'). This is not technically wrong, but it is an affected style which many academics do not like. Try to avoid this. It is better to write 'I' than 'the researcher'.

Referring to countable things as 'an amount' (e.g. 'an amount of people'). It is 'number' if it is countable and 'amount' if it is not. For example:

- There was a considerable amount of evidence.
- There was a number of incidents reported.

A similar rule applies to 'less' and 'fewer'. Use 'less' if it is uncountable and 'fewer' if it is countable. For example:

- There were fewer participants in the second survey.

- We may have less time than we think.

Using 'are' with a singular noun. This is one of the commonest (and for some people contentious) problems in written English. You will frequently see sentence like:

"A number of people are involved with this project".

"A number" is singular and this sentence should read

"A number of people is involved with this project".

Even though this may sounds wrong, it is the correct grammar. The awkwardness of the sound can be avoided by using words like "Several" or "Many" as in

- Several people are involved in this project.
-

Other examples of correct usage:

- There is a few possibilities,
- There is a variety of approaches to solving this problem.

Using footnotes (or endnotes) excessively. There is some debate about the use of footnotes which in general are either liked or strongly disliked. Those who dislike footnotes argue that they break up the continuity of the text. Those who like to use footnotes argue that they want to break up this continuity to emphasise the point they wish to make. In former times footnotes offered problems to typesetters and were unpopular with publishers for that reason. Endnotes were easier to handle typographically. Today there are no problems offered by either of these writing devices.

Overusing adverbs and adjectives. Adverbs should be used sparingly in academic writing and adjectives should be used with care. A particularly problematic adverb is 'very'. What is the difference between 'important' and 'very important'? The word 'very' normally implies that the writer is impressed with the issues being written about and this can be expressed in a better way than by the word 'very'. An example would be 'The Department's sales success was very highly regarded by the senior management' which might be written without the word 'very' as follows, 'Senior management applauded the success of the Department's sales'.

Try to avoid using it at all if you can. Colloquial expressions which need to be used sparingly and with care such as "the very idea" are exempt from this rule.

Qualifying absolutes. This is a special case of misuse of adjectives and adverbs. For example, do not write sentences like:

- It was absolutely essential.
- This is more fundamental.

Abbreviating the word 'not'. Some universities and examiners do not mind this practice, but to be on the safe side it is better to avoid abbreviations such as 'don't', 'can't', 'won't' etc.).

Writing '%' after a number. Again this is not technically incorrect, but is not considered best practice except in a table. Write '20 percent'.

Starting a sentence with a number.

Wrong: 9 managers resigned when the takeover was announced.

Right: Nine managers resigned when the takeover was announced.

Using full stops in acronyms. Do not use full stops when writing acronyms.

Wrong: He used his PH. D. (or P.H.D.) when he worked as a researcher for the U.N.O.

Right: He used his PhD when he worked as a researcher for the UNO.

Writing one sentence paragraphs. As pointed out elsewhere in this book, flow is an important concept in writing. Too many short paragraphs can make a work feel 'bitty' and are not conducive to developing a line of argument.

Referencing incorrectly. It is quite common to see references presented incorrectly. It is essential that researchers develop a thorough knowledge of the referencing system they are required to use. Some common examples of errors are:

Using parentheses when referring to what an author or authors said.

Wrong: This is confirmed by (Smith and Jones 1990).

Right: This is confirmed by Smith and Jones (1990).

Referring to authors by their full name. Refer to authors using their surname only (unless there are two authors with the same name that you need to distinguish between).

Wrong: According to Gerry Murphy (2011) most people prefer the first option.

Right: According to Murphy (2011) most people prefer the first option.

List multiple authors. You should use 'et al.' when referencing more than two authors.

Wrong: Jones, Smith, Murphy, King and Anderson (2007) claim otherwise.

Right: Jones et al. (2007) claim otherwise.

Missing page numbers when citing. Always use double quotation marks and provide the page number when you are quoting somebody else, e.g.

Smith (2009, p4) states that "most managers felt that the IT people were helpful".

and single quotes when you want to draw attention to a word or phrase, e.g.

Sometimes the possibility of 'failure' is not even acknowledged.

The above is a short list of some of the most common errors. A researcher should acquire a book on English Style or English Writing Practice and acquaint him or herself with what is considered good practice. Be careful to obtain a reference book which refers to your particular version of English. Some word processors recognise a dozen or more different versions of English.

Useful guidance on style may be obtained at:

http://ec.europa.eu/translation/english/guidelines/documents/styleguide_english_dgt_en.pdf

http://www.grammarbook.com/numbers/numbers.asp

Appendix 5 - The challenge of writing with adequate rigour without obfuscation

It is sometimes thought that writing with rigour means using an extensive and sophisticated vocabulary and employing complex syntax. While it is correct to say that academic writing, especially at doctoral level, will inevitably require some specialized vocabulary and often require non-trivial expression, it is not at all correct to say that the ideas in a dissertation need to be presented in an opaque manner. It is important to have a balance which employs rigour in writing while not slipping into obfuscation.

Obfuscation creates problems. Here are two examples which are worthy of mention. The first is when you actually have something important or useful to say. In this circumstance impenetrable prose leads to a risk of being misunderstood or, more probably, not being understood at all. This is the academic equivalent of shooting oneself in the foot. You want your examiners to grasp what you are saying and appreciate your thinking and/or insights. The second is where flowery language is used to dress up a banal point in an attempt to make it seem more profound. While the latter is, alas, an all too common practice in academia, it has no place in a PhD dissertation. Doing this will only undermine credibility with examiners.

This appendix first offers some brief extracts of writing which demand much from the reader and which are therefore not regarded as examples of writing with adequate rigour. It then gives a couple of examples of dressing up simple ideas in complicated verbal garb. With regard to the first of these, it is only fair to acknowledge that these paragraphs are offered out of the context of the whole work of which they form part and reading them in context may well assist in their understanding. Nonetheless even in context they are difficult pieces of writing to understand. The two short passages illustrate the type of writing Alan Sokal spoke of when he wrote the paragraph which follows them.

> *"This privileging of an entitative conception of reality generates an attitude that assumes the possibility and desirability of symbolically representing the diverse aspects of our phenomenal experiences using an established and atemporal repository of terms and conceptual categories for the purposes and classification and description".*

Chia R, The Production of Management Knowledge, p5, Sage, London 2002

> *"I have dwelt at some length on the exposition of the non-foundational constitution of information as difference that makes a difference because it provides the conceptual underpinning for understanding the growth of information out of information. It is unlikely that the complexity and ramifications of current information growth dynamics would be understood without serious consideration of the non-foundational constitution of information and this self-referential pattern it is associated with. To the degree, then, that contemporary computational technology overcomes the incompatibilities of older information sources that remain separate for, at least, technical reasons, it also vastly expands the potential for information growth. This leads us to the subject of the next section".*

Kallinikos J, The Consequences of Information – Institutional Implications of Technological Change, p63, Edward Elgar, Massachusetts, 2006

The first passage is more accessible then the second but neither is written in such a way that a reader is likely to have confidence in his or her full understanding of the meaning.

The second problem (and danger) is where opaque language and tortuous syntax are used to try to mask the banality of an idea. Here are just three examples. The first is from a paper in a sociology journal:

> *"The customer interfacing component of the distributive sector of the economy, due to its proclivity for positioning its interfaces on main transportation thoroughfares in urban environments, has a high consumer recognition factor".*

Translated this says that because shops are on the main streets, people are familiar with them.

Here is another example from a paper submitted to a leading journal:

> *"Authorizing environment is restricted in what can be authorized where too few stakeholders, ideologies and interests push Operational Capacity to restricted modes of operation thus circumscribing Public Value Outcomes"*

Translated into clear English this says:

> *"Powerful stakeholders can and do promote their own interests at the expense of the general public."*

Another example of tortured expression is provided by Bertram Russell in his paper, *How I Write*[9], as follows:

---

[9] http://www.davemckay.co.uk/philosophy/russell/russell.php?name= how.i.write

"Human beings are completely exempt from undesirable be-haviour-patterns only when certain prerequisites, not satis-fied except in a small percentage of actual cases, have, through some fortuitous concourse of favourable circum-stances, whether congenital or environmental, chanced to combine in producing an individual in whom many factors de-viate from the norm in a socially advantageous manner".

Russell then translates these words are follows: "All men are scoun-drels, or at any rate almost all. The men who are not must have had unusual luck, both in their birth and in their upbringing."

By hiding behind some big words and awkward (if even technically correct) syntax, it is hoped that the reader will be impressed by the great 'depth' of these statements. Notwithstanding the above ex-amples, many concepts which the academic writer needs to address are difficult and it is quite incorrect to believe that all these con-cepts may be simplified to the point that everyone could under-stand them. This would, in some cases at least, require a dumbing down to an unacceptable level. Snowdon (Evans 2003)[10] talks of the "level of acceptable abstraction" which can be understood in this context as the right level at which to pitch your dissertation for the audience that matters, in this case the examiners.

But even when the most demanding material is being addressed there are rules which the academic writer has to obey. Alan Sokal is said to have summarised these as follows:

*"What criteria of rigour are we talking about?" ask Sokol.
"Are we talking about the idea that a sentence that should mean something relatively determinate; that the words in it*

---

[10] Evans C, (2003) Managing for Knowledge; HR's Strategic Role, Ox-ford, UK, Butterworth Heinemann.

should mean something and have some relevance to the subject at hand: that there ought to be a logical argument from one sentence to another; that when you're talking about some external phenomena, the facts about these phenomena are relevant? I mean, were we upholding the minimal standards of evidence and logic that I would have thought would be taken for granted by anybody in the field."

Baggini J and Stangroom J, 2003, What Philosophers Think, p58, Continuum, London

In short, being an academic writer does not offer a licence to obfusticate. On the other hand an academic writer will not be given credit if the material is presented in a simplistic way. Einstein is attributed with the aphorism "Make everything as simple as possible, but no simpler" and that is the rule which needs to be followed by academic writers.

Appendix 6 – Bibliography

Bolker, J. (1998) Writing your dissertation in fifteen minutes a day. New York: Henry Holt and Company

Cochrane, J (2003) Between You and I: A Little Book of Bad English, Cambridge: Icon Books

Deane M & E Borg, (2011), Critical Thinking Analysis, Academic Research, Writing & Referencing, Harlow: Inside Track, Longman

Deane M, (2010), Academic Research, Writing & Referencing, Harlow: Inside Track, Longman

Graff, G, C Birkenstein & WW Norton (2005), They Say/I Say: The Moves That Matter in Academic Writing

Gillett A, A Hammond & M Martala, (2009), Successful Academic Writing, Harlow: Inside Track, Longman

Haycock, P. (2008) Cambridge Academic Content Dictionary Cambridge: New York University Press

Jupp. V, (2006) The SAGE Dictionary of Social Research Methods, London: Sage

Lynch Kennedy, M & W J Kennedy, (2008), Writing in the Disciplines: A Reader and Rhetoric for Academic Writers (6th Edition) Prentice Hall

O'Dell F, (2008), Academic vocabulary in use with answers, Cambridge University press, USA,

Swales J and C Feak, (2004), Academic Writing for Graduate Students: Essential Tasks and Skills, University of Michigan Press/ESL

Swetnam. D, Swetnam, R., (2010) Writing Your Dissertation: The Bestselling Guide to Planning, Preparing and Presenting First-Class Work (The How to Series). Oxford: How to books Ltd.

Truss, L. (2003) Eats, Shoots and Leaves. Profile Books,London

Appendix 7 - Some More Useful Web Tools

There are many websites which offer useful information which can assist a research degree candidate with his or her dissertation or thesis. However be aware that there are other websites which offer to have your dissertation or thesis written for you. It is not legitimate for you to use any of these facilities. Do not under any circumstances have anything to do with these websites. It is unacceptable to obtain assistance in this way and if you are found to have so done you will almost certainly find yourself before the university's disciplinary procedures.

There are hundreds if not thousands of search engines which are not as well known as the market leaders but which may be helpful under different circumstances. To access these simply search for 'search engines' in the usual way. Two search engines which may be of particular interest are:-

www.Spezify.com

http://www.dogpile.com

www.wolframalfa.com

Other websites that may be helpful are:-

http://www.theses.com/

pareonline.net/pdf/v14n13.pdf

http://writingcenter.unc.edu/resources/handouts-demos/specific-writing-assignments/dissertations

http://owl.english.purdue.edu/owl/

http://dspace.mit.edu/handle/1721.1/7582

http://www.ull.ac.uk/resources/theses.shtml

There are many more websites to be explored by readers.

Appendix 8 – Glossary

Acknowledgment: In dissertation writing it is important for the author to state the names of the individuals from whom he or she has received help or encouragement. This is normally done under a separate heading at the beginning of the work.

Action research: An approach to research where the researcher deliberately tries to change the activities or processes routinely conducted by the research participants and/or their organisation.

Anonymisation: One of the principles of academic research is that data should not be directly connectable to individual informants. The process of ensuring that the data cannot reveal the identity of the informant who supplied it is called anonymisation. A questionnaire can be relatively easily anonymised by removing any aspect which can be traced back to the person who completed it. However it is sometimes much more difficult to anonymise the results of an interview as the person's identity is sometimes apparent by the type of organisation in which he or she works as well as by his or her job description. Researchers are required to make their best efforts to anonymise data soon after it has been received.

Argument: A series of logical steps which lead to a position from which a belief or a theory is accepted.

Case study: An umbrella term which refers to the use of a group of research methods which are used to investigate a contemporary complex situation where the boundaries between the situation and its environment are not clear.

Certificates of own work: In presenting the dissertation which describes the research conducted for a research degree it is customary for the research degree candidate to certify that the work which is described in the dissertation has been done by him or her.

Code of ethics: A list of the behaviours which are expected as well as a list of the behaviours which are prohibited by the group subscribing to the code.

Data: A stimulus to any of the five senses which the researcher believes will help answer the research question. Data has to be distinguished from noise which is also a stimulus but which will not facilitate the answering of the research question.

Data Analysis: The phase in the research process where the data collected is considered, processed and tested / assessed for meaning in terms of an hypothesis, proposition, theory or the formulation of a new theory.

Data Collection: The stage in the research where the data required for the research is obtained using a preselected protocol.

Data types: There is a variety of data types but for the purposes of this book only qualitative and quantitative data are considered.

Data responsibility: The possession of personal data about informants as well as a record of the opinions of informants need to be treated with care as they could lead to some harm being done to the informant. Where this data is held by a researcher it is the researcher's responsibility to ensure that the data is protected and is not used inappropriately.

Dissertation: This word is often used synonymously with the word thesis to describe the documents which are submitted at the end of a research degree or as a component of a taught degree. For doctoral level research it is often many thousand words in length and describes the research and the finding(s). Also see **Thesis**.

Empiricism: An approach to research which relies on primary data. The basis of empiricism is based on sensed perception. Thus the researcher needs to observe the phenomenon which is being studied. This observation can be through the eyes of others. An extreme empiricist would assert that particle physics cannot be competently studied as atomic particles cannot in the normal course of events be observed. Few people would take this extreme position as they would agree that the existence of atomic particles may be known through the results of experimentation.

Ethics: A set of expected behaviours which are required if an individual is to work within or along with a group. Honesty, professionalism and care not to do harm to others are the hallmarks for a code of ethics.

Focus Groups: A group of individuals which has been assembled so that the researcher can observe a discussion about the research question. The individuals need to be knowledgeable about the subject of the research and a facilitator needs to keep the discussion on track. Focus groups should consist of between 4 and 6 participants and their duration should be between 45 minutes and 90 minutes.

Generalisable: The ability to claim that a research finding is applicable to other locations and instances than the one at which the research was conducted. Research finding are sometimes thought to be either generalisable or not generalisable whereas in reality research findings may be in some respects generalisable and in other respects not.

Grounded theory: Grounded theory is an inductive, theory discovery methodology that allows the researcher to develop a theoretical account of the general features of a topic/ situation while simultaneously grounding the account in empirical observations or data - Glaser, B. and Strauss, A. (1967) The Discovery of Grounded Theory: Strategies for Qualitative Research. Aldine, New York.

Harm: Someone or some organisation has been done harm if they are physically, intellectually, emotionally, financially, by reputation, or in some other way worse off than they were before the harm was done.

Harvard referencing system: A system which facilitates a reader accessing original material from which ideas or quotations have been found and used. The main characteristics of the Harvard referencing system is that the author's name and the date of publication are inserted in the text where the idea or quotation is used and a list of all the references used in the work is provided in alphabetical order are the end of the work.

Hermeneutics: The word is derived from the Greek word Hermes which was the name of a messenger used by the gods to communicate with each other and with humans. Hermeneutics is a tradition dating back to the 19th century of the study of the theory of interpretation and the practice thereof. It includes both verbal and non-verbal communications. Hermeneutics draws on a number of different frameworks including alethic, critical, double, etc.

Hypothesis: A claim made by a researcher which requires testing to see if it may be rejected. An hypothesis needs to be stated in such a way that it may be rejected.

Hypothesis testing: The way in which researchers attempt to refute an hypothesis. An hypothesis test will involve a Null Hypothesis and an Alternative Hypothesis. If the Null Hypothesis is rejected then the Alternative Hypothesis is accepted.

Hypothetico-deductive: This term is used as a synonym for positivist or quantitative research which is based on deduction and the testing of hypotheses obtained there from.

Informant: An individual who supplies a researcher with information which may contribute to answering the research question. See Respondent.

Interpretivism: An approach to research which does not rely heavily on numbers where the researcher attempts to study the situation through his or her own eyes and through the eyes of informants.

Likert Scale: Named after Rensis Likert, a founder of the University of Michigan's Institute for Social Research, the Likert Scale is a psychometric measure which is frequently used in questionnaires and is the most commonly used scale in survey research. When completing a Likert Scale questionnaire participants answer in levels of agreement with a statement. Each question within one of these questionnaires is referred to as a Likert item, although it usually appears to be a scale of itself, and a Likert Scale is the sum of a number of Likert items. Likert items may be graduated using 5, 7 or 9 positions of difference. It is however common to have an odd number of positions. The mid-position is regarded as neither supporting nor disagreeing with the proposition. Sometimes a forced opinion is gained by removing the mid-position. After completion of the questionnaire the responses can be analysed individually or summed up to create a score for the group. This group score is a Likert Scale, and can be treated as interval data.

Management guidelines: The advice provided to professional practising managers and executives as a result of the research question being answered. This provides one of the bases for the justification of research in business and management studies.

Mixed methods: An approach to academic research which employs aspects of both positivism and interpretivism.

Monograph: The reporting of one large piece of work which may be presented for examination for the award of a research degree. A monograph is contrasted with a series of peer reviewed papers which most universities and business schools will also accept for the awarding of a research degree.

Name date system: This is another name for the Harvard Referencing System.

Outsourcing: The use of outsiders to conduct some aspect of the research on behalf of the primary researcher.

Plagiarism: This refers to the use of the ideas or words of others without adequate attribution. Plagiarism is considered by academics to be a violation of the trust which academics have in each other. Increasingly, universities are requiring students to submit an electronic copy of their work so that it may be tested for plagiarism.

Positivism: An approach to research which usually seeks to establish cause and effect relationships. Deduction and the use of numeric data are the most commonplace ways in which positivism is practised. Positivism underpins much of the research conducted today in business and management studies, although there is an increase in the role of interpretivism.

Pragmatism: A philosophical position taken by researchers which was named by Charles Sanders Peirce in which what works is in some sense right; also, what is useful is 'true' or right. This philosophy was further developed by William James and John Dewey. According to the pragmatists the practice of inquiry is a social activity. There is always a problem behind research. Research is a problem solver. Research is a transaction – an ongoing state of inquiry with changing evidence and changes in what we could consider as evidence. Warranted assertions, competent inquiry and knowledge are outputs of the research. An important test of validity in business and management research is whether the findings are regarded by the community interested in the research as being useful. As such, pragmatism is an important aspect of validating business, and management studies research requires the application of the ideas of the pragmatists.

Primary researcher: The individual who is responsible to the Ethics Committee for the conduct of the research. May also be referred to as the lead researcher.

Qualitative data: Aspects or dimensions which do not rely exclusively on numeric scores or evaluations. Qualitative data will usually be in the form of words and pictures. It could also involve sounds, tastes and vision. In as far as qualitative data is used to describe phenomena, numbers in the form of tables and graphs may also constitute qualitative data.

Quantitative data: The use of numbers as a description. Numbers which represent the dimensions of a phenomenon or the number of times an occurrence happens.

Questionnaire: A data collection instrument which contain a list of questions. The questions may be a collection of highly structured issues requiring a *tick the box* type reply or it may contain open ended questions in which the informant may supply his or her own comments.

Reflection: Standing back from the research and contemplating what it means to the researcher and to others.

Research design: The plan created by the researcher by which he or she intends to answer the research question in a convincing manner for the award of a research degree.

Research participant: See Informant.

Respondent: See Informant.

Scholarly activity: An activity which is conducted in an erudite manner based on rigorous intellectual analysis and dedicated to high ethical standards and conduct.

Sponsor: The entity, organisation or in some cases the individual who funds the research. In academic research the sponsor could be the Head of Department or Head of School who has agreed to be responsible for finding the necessary funding for the research.

Termination: When the research undertaken ceases it is considered to have been terminated. Reasons for this vary but it may include individual persons taking part in the research changing their mind about contributing to the research, finding themselves in a conflict of interest, or sponsors of the research or Research Ethics Committees withdrawing their approval of the research.

Theoretical research: An approach to research which is conducted using secondary data and discourse among knowledgeable students, faculty or other individuals. Theoretical research does not employ primary data.

Thesis: In academe there are two distinct meanings to the word thesis. It is a scholarly report based on an original piece of research required for many post graduate university degrees (and sometimes undergraduate degrees) and for all doctoral degrees awarded by universities. The word thesis also refers to the new theory which is contained in such a report.

Triangulation: A research technique which requires obtaining a number of difference sources of data. The different sources may be related to different individuals or different types of documents or a different theoretical lens through which data may be viewed.

Verbatim quotations: This refers to the use of the exact words written or spoken by an authority or an informant.

Version control: When data is transferred from the notes of the researcher or from a recording made by the researcher it may take several days to complete. This work needs to be controlled in order to prevent or at least minimise the number of errors which can creep into this type of work. Version control refers to the researcher's ability to know exactly what has been done and what additional work is still required.

Writer's block: Sometimes a researcher may find that he or she encounters an unusual level of difficulty in writing their research. This is sometimes referred to as writer's block. Writer's block may be a temporary problem lasting hours or a few days. In other cases it can be more serious and persist for weeks or even months.

Index

parsimony, 12, 67, 90
photographs, i, 19, 20, 77, 78
plagiarism, 68, 92, 118
plagiarism testing, 68
portfolio, 86, 87, 88, 89
positivist, 15, 41, 54, 116
pragmatist, 40, 41
Proofreading, i, 24, 26
proposition, 57, 114, 117
protocol, ii, 6, 76, 114
published, iii, v, 6, 7, 9, 10, 32—36, 39, 42, 43, 73, 74, 78, 84—88, 91, 92
qualitative data, 41, 42, 43, 45, 58, 59, 80, 119
quantitative data, 42, 43, 58, 80, 114
questionnaire, 41, 42, 43, 49, 50, 52, 64, 98, 113, 117
Questionnaire, 119
realist, 40, 41
reductio ad absurdum, 53
reflections, iii, 63, 94
replication, 45
research design, 39, 48, 98
Research Ethics Committee, 120
research protocol, 6, 73, 76
research report, 1
Respondent, 117, 119
route to the doctorate, iii, 87, 92
seminal, 32, 34, 35
simplistic, 12, 13, 108
social constructivist, 40
story, 13, 14, 19, 54, 59, 98
style, 11, 12, 17, 19, 26, 27, 38, 80, 88, 93, 99, 103
summary transcripts, 52
supervisor, iv, 8, 10, 23, 26, 30, 31, 69, 70, 71, 73, 88, 89, 92, 98